Cumberland by the Blackstone

250 YEARS OF HERITAGE

Cumberland by the Blackstone
250 YEARS OF HERITAGE

by David W. Balfour

and Joyce Hindle Koutsogiane, Ed.D.

Title page photo: Our Lady of the Valley Monastery Church

Endsheet photo: The Village of Berkeley in Cumberland, Rhode Island, from a postcard circa 1908, from collection of Joseph E. Coduri

Copyright © 1997 by the Town of Cumberland, Rhode Island
Expanded second edition 2006

The Donning Company Publishers
184 Business Park Drive, Suite 206
Virginia Beach, VA 23462

Steve Mull, General Manager
Barbara Buchanan, Office Manager
Elizabeth B. Bobbitt, Executive Editor
Jamie R. Watson, Reprint Editor
L. J. Wiley, Graphic Designer
Lynn Parrott, Reprint Graphic Designer
Monica F. Oglesby, Imaging Artist
Amy Thomann, Reprint Imaging Artist
Scott Rule, Director of Marketing
Stephanie Linneman, Marketing Coordinator
Susan Adams, Reprint Project Research Coordinator

Mary Taylor, Reprint Project Director

Library of Congress Cataloging-in-Publication Data

Balfour, David W.
   Cumberland by the Blackstone: 250 years of heritage / by David W. Balfour and Joyce Hindle Koutsogiane.
      p.   cm.
   Includes bibliographical references (p.) and index.
   ISBN-13: 978-1-57864-357-8 (hard cover: alk. paper)
   ISBN-10: 1-57864-357-0 (hard cover: alk. paper)
   1. Cumberland (R.I. : Town)—History. 2. Cumberland (R.I. : Town)—History—Pictorial works. I. Koutsogiane, Joyce Hindle. II. Title.
   F89.C93B5   1997
   974.5'2—dc21   97-35818
                CIP

Printed in the United States of America by Walsworth Publishing Company

TABLE OF CONTENTS

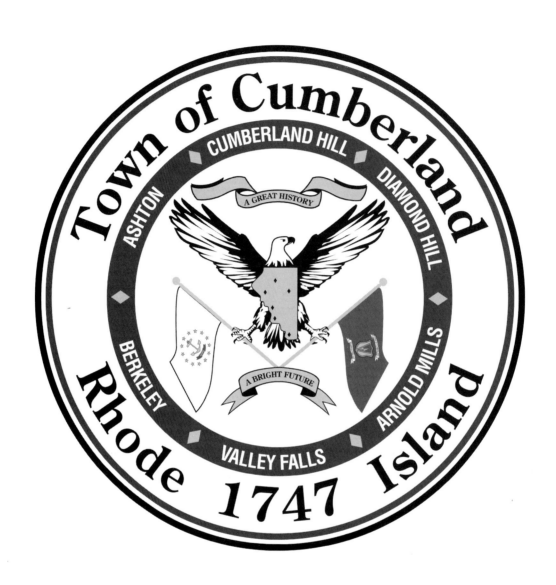

PREFACE

n 1997, when the Town of Cumberland, Rhode Island, celebrated its 250th anniversary, the first edition of *Cumberland by the Blackstone: 250 Years of Heritage* was published. Response to the book was beyond all expectations and the public demand to republish it was not surprising. In the nine years since our initial publication, many changes have taken place. There is new leadership at the Town Council level and the executive office in the Town Hall has had new occupants.

With the help of the Rhode Island Department of Environmental Management, the Rhode Island Department of Transportation, and the John H. Chafee Blackstone River Valley National Heritage Corridor Commission, the new bicycle path along the banks of the Blackstone River has come into use, and the long abandoned Pratt Dam, in the woods behind the site of what once was the Lonsdale Sports Arena, now provides hikers and bikers an opportunity to enjoy some of the town's scenic beauty.

The acquisition of what once was farmland has allowed Cumberland to provide residents and visitors an opportunity to enjoy open fields. The former Franklin dairy farm on Abbott Run Valley Road will offer wider possibilities for passive recreation.

New homes, many at the executive level, have been built since our initial publication, and new families have expressed an interest in learning about our town's history. The desire to recognize historic preservation as a means of educating future citizens seems to be foremost among Cumberland residents.

It is the hope that this updated second edition will allow a new generation of Cumberland residents to face the future, reminded that the town's colorful past is a stepping stone to an even more vibrant future.

ACKNOWLEDGMENTS

t is with great thanks that we acknowledge the following people for their contributions to the creation of this book. For being the impetus behind the original project, we would like to thank the former mayor of the Town of Cumberland, Edgar R. Alger III. We are most grateful to Darlene M. Guerin, Edmond H. Guerin, Jr., and Joseph E. Coduri for sharing their extensive postcard collections with us. Photos submitted by the Rowbottom family were taken by the late Robert Rowbottom. The photos were not only in excellent condition, but were also excellent artistic representatives of a bygone time. We also gratefully acknowledge the contribution of Norman Galipeau and his photography studio, Exposure One, as our photo reproduction expert. Many thanks to Christine Maino, Paula Mekdsy, and Robert Snow for their contributions. Special appreciation should be extended to Cumberland's present mayor, Hon. David Iwuc, and the members of the current Town Council. For their time and patience, we would also like to thank our friends and families. For the long list of people for whom the time and space do not permit for thanking them here, please know that we are truly grateful.

Award-winning photo shot by Albert Maurer about 1920. Courtesy of Louise Potter.

INTRODUCTION

The State of Rhode Island and Providence Plantations is the smallest state with the longest name in the United States of America. Founded by religious dissenters from the Massachusetts Bay Colony, Rhode Islanders have been at the forefront of independent thinking throughout their colorful history. The residents of the Town of Cumberland were no exception, having carved a place for themselves and the town in the annals of history.

To understand the town, it is advantageous to know more about the state. It was Rhode Islanders who burned a British revenue schooner (the *Gaspee* on June 9, 1772) eighteen months before Massachusetts' patriots threw tea into Boston's harbor. The stalwart people of Rhode Island declared their independence from Great Britain on May 4, 1776, two months before the other colonies. Interestingly, Rhode Island was the last state to ratify the United States Constitution in 1790. While Rhode Island had declared slavery illegal in 1652, over two hundred years before the rest of the United States, many residents still participated actively in the slave trade. However, abolitionists Samuel Hopkins and Ezra Stiles (who later served as president of Yale University) helped enact a ban on slave trading in 1774, the first such law in the colonies. Further evidence of the independent thinking of the Rhode Island people was that it was one of only two states in the country to reject the Volstead Act (Prohibition). Indeed, many Rhode Islanders made their fortunes through "rum-running" during the 1920s.

"Give Me Another Worm, Jimmy!" A prize winning photo by Robert Rowbottom, Ashton Photographer, taken along the Blackstone River in 1916.

Rhode Island is a state of many firsts. It had the first recorded strike by working women in America. (This occurred in the city of Pawtucket in 1824 by textile weavers.) Rhode Island has the oldest Jewish House of Worship in North America (the Touro Synagogue in Newport), the oldest Quaker meetinghouse in America (Friends Meeting House, also in Newport), the first water-powered textile mill (Slater Mill in Pawtucket), and the nation's first discount department store (Ann and Hope Department Store in Cumberland). Rhode Island's proud heritage also includes the fourth largest marble dome without skeletal support in the world (its state house in Providence), America's first Baptist Church (located in Providence) and the carousel now recognized as the oldest carousel in America (Flying Horses in Westerly). The town of Bristol, Rhode Island, sponsors the oldest Fourth of July Parade in America, celebrating Independence Day since 1786.

Other significant Rhode Island facts include that the town of Portsmouth, Rhode Island, founded by Ann Hutchinson in 1638, was the first community in this country to have been founded by a woman. Pelham Street in Newport was the first gas lighted street in America. The Washington Trust Company in Westerly was the first bank to issue currency bearing a portrait of George Washington. Peace Dale in South County was the site of the first power loom in the country.

Further interesting information about the Town of Cumberland is that the Manville Mill, which spanned the Blackstone River dividing Cumberland and Lincoln, was the largest mill under one roof in the world, until it burned in the 1950s. Jeremiah Wilkinson from the Town of Cumberland made the first hand-hewn nail in the colonies (in 1775) and is reputed to have been the first person in America to "draw" wire. Oziel Wilkinson, Jeremiah's father, made the first wing gudgeon in America. The second cotton mill in the United States was erected by Elisha Waterman in 1799 at Robin Hollow in Cumberland. With such contributions by its citizens, the state of Rhode Island and Providence Plantations has been called the "Birthplace of the Industrial Revolution."

The first non-Native American settler in the area now known as Cumberland, Rhode Island, was William Blackstone who in 1634 settled on land which borders the river that now bears his name. He arrived two years before Roger Williams settled the capital city of Providence. As Cumberland was still at that time located within the state of Massachusetts, however, it is Williams who is credited with the founding of the state of Rhode Island. Both men had come to the area to escape the religious restrictions of the Puritan Colony of Massachusetts.

In the nineteenth century, Rhode Island was one of the largest producers of textiles in the country. During those years, the industry had drawn thousands of immigrants from Canada, Ireland, England, and Italy. Today their descendants make up the bulk of the state's population. The state became a leader in the manufacturing of jewelry during the second half of the 1900s based on its perfection of a process of plating metals in the 1700s.

Rhode Island's nickname is the "Ocean State" for the miles of beautiful coastline which make the state a summer vacation paradise. Narragansett Bay is the second largest estuary (after the Chesapeake Bay) on the Eastern seacoast. The seaport of Newport became the summer haven for the rich during the opulent period of the late 1880s through the 1900s. Many of the mansions are now open to the public. Rhode Island is also the home of Trinity Square Repertory Company, a nationally recognized theatre company, and the Roger Williams Park Zoo, an active participant in an international program for the preservation of endangered species. Both are located in the capital city of Providence, the third largest city in New England.

The history of any town begins with a journey. In the case of Cumberland, the journey began as one of religious freedom. It was the travel of William Blackstone that established the area which would ultimately, in 1747, become the Town of Cumberland, a part of Providence County, in the State of Rhode Island and Providence Plantations. The town has made many contributions to the state. Its citizens, both past and present, are highlighted in the following history.

*William Blackstone made his home
on the shores of the beautiful Blackstone River
shown here around 1907 going over one of its many
dams. Postcard courtesy of the Rowbottom family.*

PART I

A History of Cumberland

The Town of Cumberland is unique in that the land which it occupies was the home of the first European settler in Rhode Island. It was to "The Wilderness" that the Reverend William Blackstone (also spelled Blaxton) fled in 1634 from Shawmut, the peninsula of the Massachusetts Bay Colony which is now the City of Boston. He had originally settled around 1625 on what is now Boston Common, an area that was then shoreline. It provided a quiet refuge for this scholarly Anglican cleric who wished only to be alone with his books, his garden, his cattle, and his thoughts.

Around 1634 Puritans settled on nearby Shawmut Peninsula. They found the water from their wells to have a high sulfur content, so they asked Blackstone to share his rather substantial acreage with them. Not unlike what might happen today when a developer builds new homes on what once was a grazing pasture, the Puritans began to dictate a "neighborhood policy" with which Blackstone was expected to comply. He refused. On his departure from Boston, Blackstone is reported to have stated: "I left England to get from under the power of the Lord Bishops, but in America, I am fallen under the Lord Brethren. I looked to have dwelt with my orchards and my books, and my young fawn and bull in undisturbed solitude. Was there not room enough for all of thee? Could ye not leave the hermit in his corner?" He sold his land to his neighbors, and according to old records, the town laid out a plan for a "trayning field." That field, the present Boston Common, is still in use for that purpose.

Legend has it that Blackstone's principal conveyance was a white brindle bull, and when he and his bull had proceeded into the wilderness for about fifty miles, he located a terraced hill which sloped to a river. It was here, at the site of the Ann and Hope Mill, that the first European settler in what is now the Town of Cumberland, made his home. He called his house "Study Hall" and the hill on which it stood "Study Hill."

Blackstone lived alone at Study Hall where he tended his gardens and apple trees (he is credited with the establishment of the yellow sweeting variety of apple on this continent) until July 4, 1659. On that date, he journeyed to Boston and was married to Sarah Stevenson, a widow considerably younger than himself. They had one child, a son named John.

An early photo showing the agrarian nature of early Cumberland dates from around 1900. Courtesy of Jean Schofield Madden.

William Blackstone died in 1675 and the Blackstone house and library were burned by the natives during King Philip's War (1675–1676). Study Hill was leveled in the nineteenth century to create the mill. Descendents of William Blackstone live today in the Town of Branford, Connecticut, where a memorial library honors descendants. Blackstone's grave in Cumberland has been marked by a simple monument, located near the approximate site of his homestead. His actual remains, however, have been lost in the many years and changing ownership of the property in the area of Study Hill.

Although Blackstone had ownership of the land by what would be called today, "squatters rights" there was never a record of his ever being given title to the land by various Native American tribes who inhabited the area, some of whom referred to him in the deeds as "The old man at Pawtucket."

There was no public record of him by name until 1661 when all of what is now Cumberland, and several other towns in both Rhode Island and Massachusetts as well, were deeded by Wamsetta (also called Alexander), Chief Sachem of Pokanokett, to Captain Thomas Willett of Wannamoisett. One of the bounds of this deed, called the Rehoboth North Purchase, refers to a place called " . . . by the natives *Wawepoonseag* [translated: the place where birds are taken], where one Blackstone now sojourneth." This is the first official record of any transaction concerning the land now known as Cumberland.

The Ann and Hope Mill, shown in a postcard around 1900, was constructed by the Lonsdale Company and occupies the area that was Blackstone's home. The construction of the mill and its many buildings caused the loss of the remains of Blackstone. Courtesy of Darlene M. and Edmond H. Guerin, Jr.

Together with a small portion of Attleboro, which had been referred to as "The Gore," the Massachusetts towns of Warren, Bristol, Tiverton, and Little Compton were all annexed to Rhode Island by an act of the Rhode Island General Assembly on January 27, 1747. The Gore was incorporated into a township named Cumberland with the signature of John Bartlett, Esquire, signing the document for the town. Most of the occupants of the area were originally from Great Britain. Since in 1646, William, Duke of Cumberland, defeated Prince Charles of Scotland ("Bonnie Prince Charlie"), at Culloden Moor in Scotland, pro British sentiment ran high, the new town was named "Cumberland" in honor of the Duke.

Cumberland is situated in the northeast corner of the state, about ten miles from the capital city of Providence. Its triangular shape is bounded on the east by Massachusetts, on the north by the city of Woonsocket, and on the west by the Blackstone River which also separates the town from the Town

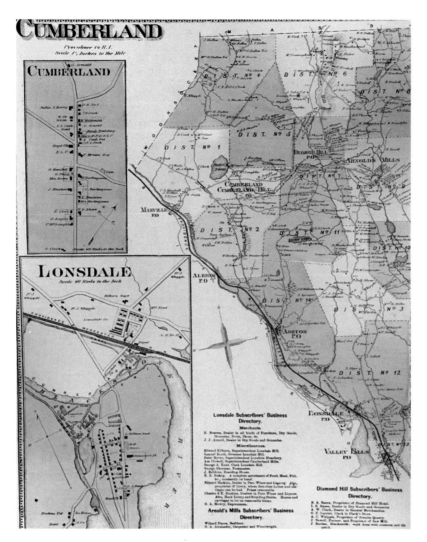

CUMBERLAND

of Lincoln, Rhode Island. Cumberland's southernmost boundary lies on the city lines of Pawtucket and Central Falls. The last boundary change was in 1867, when the village of Woonsocket Falls was removed from Cumberland became the City of Woonsocket.

Cumberland is 28.64 square miles in area. Before being settled by the English, the inhabitants were the Native American tribes of Narragansetts, Nipmucks, and Wampanoags who hunted in the vast forests of white oak, red oak, red maple, gray birch, American chestnut, hickory, and white pine. The land is also known for its interesting geological features

An 1870 map of Cumberland shows the early residents' homesteads. Many descendants of these residents live in the town today. Courtesy of Gordon Carr.

The Gatehouse at Ashton in a 1907 postcard illustrates the many ponds and waterways located in Cumberland. Great glaciers carved and gouged the ponds as they made their way to the sea. Courtesy of Joseph E. Coduri.

This beautiful scene shows Diamond Hill, a great source of granite and ore utilized in local industry and construction. Courtesy of Jean Schofield Madden.

and is rich in a variety of minerals which in earlier times made it a major source of ore for iron production. The stone known as Cumberlandite has been named for its only location verified in the world: Iron Mine Hill in Cumberland. The town's generally fertile soil makes it a good spot for gardens and historically made it one of the state's major farming communities, although today few working farms remain. The earliest known road in Cumberland is what is known today as Mendon Road, constructed in 1650 in a north-south direction from the Village of Valley Falls to the Mendon, Massachusetts, line.

Many rivers and streams which are tributary to the Blackstone River make the northern part of the town an ideal spot for construction of two reservoirs which now constitute the water supply for the city of Pawtucket and parts of Cumberland. The Blackstone River greatly influenced industrial development along its banks. Smaller streams, which include the Abbott Run, Monastery Brook, Scott Brook, and Sneech Brook,

The Arnold Mills area spawned a great many small mills and other businesses including boatmaking. Proximity to water was advantageous in this industry. 1910 postcard courtesy of Darlene M. and Edmond H. Guerin, Jr.

Idyllic Miscoe Lake is located in the northeastern part of the town. Postcard from around 1910, courtesy of Eleanor Johnson.

eventually feed into the river, and contributed to that development. They are connected by a series of wetlands and swamps such as Ash Swamp, Pine Swamp, and Burnt Swamp. The building of the reservoirs encouraged the forming of dams to harness energy with which to run local industry. Several ponds were created by these dams: Rawson Pond and Howard Pond in the northern part of Cumberland, and Robin Hollow Pond and Happy Hollow Pond in the southern part. Sneech Pond and Little Pond are natural lakes. Sneech Pond became part of the town's water supply in the 1930s.

The first town meeting was held in February of 1747 for the purpose of electing town officers and deputies to the General Assembly. The meeting also transacted other business consistent with the organization of a town government. Job

Bartlett was chosen town moderator and town clerk and, together with Israel Whipple and Samuel Peck, were elected deputies to represent the town in the Rhode Island General Assembly. Job Bartlett, Joseph Brown, David Whipple, Jacob Bartlett, Jr., Nathaniel Ballou, and William Walcott were named as town councilmen. Samuel Bartlett was selected to be the first town treasurer. Descendents of these early settlers still live in Cumberland today.

The Ballou family settled in the northern part of Cumberland in the late 1690s. It was this family that erected a Six Principle Baptist Meeting House (in 1749) which stood for years on Elder Ballou Meeting House Road until it was destroyed by vandals in the 1960s. Originally named for its first pastor, Elder Cook, it was renamed for Elder Abner Ballou, pastor from 1775 to 1806. It was located near Iron Mine Hill from which ore was mined to create cannons used during the French and Indian War.

The descendants of Walter Cook came to Cumberland from Mendon, Massachusetts. The Whipples were among the first to settle in the area of Diamond Hill. The Tower family

Elder Ballou Meeting House was the first house of worship in Cumberland. Built in 1749, it was destroyed by vandals during the 1960s. 1908 Postcard courtesy of Darlene M. and Edmond H. Guerin, Jr.

The interior of the Elder Ballou Meeting House showing its simple and sturdy furnishings. Postcard circa 1910, courtesy of Jane Wood.

settled near Diamond Hill on what is now Tower Hill Road. The Razee and Tingley families also had large land holdings in the area. The Arnold family operated a mill in the village of East Cumberland (now called Arnold Mills) where the Metcalfs operated forges and furnaces. Inventive genius and creativity as a family, made the Wilkinsons legends in the state and nation far beyond the small village of Ashton. Many more families and their descendants have had great influence on the development of the town as it is today.

Little doubt exists that most of the land that now encompasses the Town of Cumberland was agrarian in nature, but in the mid-seventeenth century things began to change. Monied interests in Massachusetts Bay Colony began to take notice of the fact that iron ore had been found in the gore of land that existed near Attleboro. Iron Mine Hill and the area of Diamond Hill were the principal locations of the ore.

By the mid-eighteenth century, census figures listed 806 permanent inhabitants in the town (1748 figures). By 1774 this number had increased to 1,756 inhabitants, Many of whom were farmers. Most farms were small and operated to provide basic crops and livestock for the family's consumption. By 1750, the number of farms in the town necessitated the creation of a town pound in the area near the present Cumberland High School on Mendon Road. The farms were connected by a series of country lanes bordered by stone walls which later became the first town roads. Well preserved sections of these original walks can be found along Tower Hill Road and parts of West Wrentham Road.

Welcome to Ashton! This old village of Cumberland, like many other villages, had its roots in farming. This 1910 postcard shows Ashton life as it once was. Few working farms still exist in the much changed countryside of Cumberland. Courtesy of Scott Welton.

Aside from agriculture, a principal industry in the town was iron production. The Blackstone River and its primary tributary in Cumberland, Abbott Run, provided the waterpower to keep the furnaces running. Town records indicate that several blast furnaces were in existence in the town. The construction of water powered furnaces, which were constantly in blast, created the iron from the ore which could later be transformed not only into utensils, but also into cannon for military use.

During the nineteenth century, Cumberland's industry and transportation developments dramatically changed the nature

Welcome to Diamond Hill! Its villages and farms sit in the shadow of the majestic landmark known for its variety of rare minerals. 1917 postcard courtesy of Scott Welton.

Farming was an essential first industry to Cumberland families. This photo illustrates the continuation of this tradition through the early 1930s in the small village in Ashton. Photo by Robert Rowbottom, courtesy of Kenneth Rowbottom.

Haywagons were an integral part of the Cumberland farm. Photo circa early 1900s, courtesy of Eva Schofield.

The New York/New Haven and Hartford Railroad took over control of the former Providence/Worcester Railroad in town. The repair shop was located in Valley Falls on Maple Street off Broad Street. Photo circa 1920, courtesy of Mary Wood.

of the town from a small farming community to a number of villages with their own separate identities. The arrival of railroads into the town in 1847 opened the possibilities of commerce with Providence and Worcester. Passenger service continued until the 1940s with limited freight service continuing today.

By 1800 Cumberland's population had grown to 2,056 and in 1865, it was 8,216. By the end of the nineteenth century, the growth in population had created a need for better public services. The Cumberland Street Railway Company, incorporated in the 1870s, operated horse cars from Valley Falls to Cumberland Hill. These in turn were updated in the 1890s with an electric streetcar system.

In 1828 the Tillinghast Law was passed by the Rhode Island General Assembly which established the free school system. By the end of the year, Cumberland had thirteen district schools in the individual villages. The Pound School which was built in 1830 was used until 1925. Other schools

The railroad at Arnold Mills Station. Each village was served by the railroad for passenger and freight service well into the 1900s. Schoolchildren road the train to the high school in Valley Falls from all over Cumberland. Photo circa 1900, courtesy of Evan Schofield.

bore the names of residents of the town: Ballou, Tingley, Razee, Cargill, Jenkes, and Clark. The schools were old houses remodeled for the purpose or built specifically as one-room schoolhouses. They were heated by fireplaces or by iron stoves with the help of the older boys who served as janitors. Some families furnished the wood for the stoves instead of giving money to support the school. By 1860 other schools such as Tower Hill, Grant, Kent, and Plain were also operating in the town. Salaries at that time ranged from $16 to $24 per month for teachers.

In 1894 the first town-wide school system was created following the passage of a state act requiring the abolishment of

The trolley to Woonsocket is seen in this picture from around 1920. The introduction of the automobile put electric cars out of business, but trolleys traversed the whole length of the town until late in the 1940s. Courtesy of Walter Gelinas.

The John Street Trolley, circa 1920, is shown in a photo courtesy of Water Gelinas.

individual school districts. There were sixteen grammar schools in the town in 1894. In 1889 the first Cumberland High School opened on the spot where the B. F. Norton Elementary School now stands on Broad Street in Valley Falls. Two teachers taught the fifty students at the high school level in three courses: Classical, Latin-English (a four year program) and English (a three year business course).

The first two school buses, delivered to the town in 1921 and 1924, were driven by Percy A. Schofield and Lyman Richardson. The buses were trucks adapted for the purpose. One had actually been confiscated from rum runners in Tiverton and sold to the Town of Cumberland, complete with a bullet hole in the driver's side door. Students tell stories of having to crowd into the back of the bus to assist the driver in getting the bus out of the mud. The advent of bus service eventually brought about the end of the one-room schoolhouses, as evidenced by the building of four- to six-room brick

Take the trolley through Cumberland! This 1906 postcard illustrates the impact that this form of transportation had in the town. Courtesy of Scott Welton.

The one-room schoolhouse was the tradition of the individual villages in Cumberland until a townwide system of education necessitated larger schools. This is the Arnold Mills Schoolhouse around 1900. Courtesy of William Rhodes (Rhody) Franklin.

Some buildings were multi-faceted, serving as both church and school. Courtesy of William Rhodes (Rhody) Franklin, circa 1920s.

The Lonsdale School is shown in 1904. Courtesy of Mrs. John Sherlock .

The Chapel Four Corner School, shown around 1890, was later incorporated into the church that was built near the site. Photo courtesy of Stuart Follett.

schools in various villages from the 1920s onward (e.g. Central Grammar, Community, Garvin, and Edgemere Schools). Prior to the motorized vehicles, carriages helped bring students to schools in Berkeley and Valley Falls. Pupils in the high school located in Valley Falls were brought there by railroad and electric car. The villages continued to retain a strong agricultural identity through the 1800s. Indeed most of the housing areas among the mill villages were separated by country fields even as late as the 1890s.

The remnants of what could be considered the earliest industrial development in Cumberland are found near the

The Valley Falls High School, constructed in 1889, graduated its first class in 1897. Sixteen young people graduated in that ceremony held in the town hall of the Cumberland Town House. 1909 postcard courtesy of Gordon Carr.

This was one of the first school buses, a carriage driven by Alfred Franklin in the 1890s. Courtesy of Eleanor Johnson.

The first Cumberland School Bus served the area of Community School. This bus was a 1920 Dodge with a bus body installed on it in 1924. Owner/operator Percy A. Schofield carried seventy-one children divided into two groups for separate trips. Courtesy of Jean Schofield Madden.

village of Arnold Mills, which was formerly referred to as "East Cumberland." It was here in 1735 that a group of people from the Boston area established a blast furnace for the purpose of extracting iron from rock. The Furnace Carolina, named for the wife of England's King George I, was located on the banks of the Abbott Run in the Arnold Mills area. The exact location is on private property and inaccessible to the public. There were also other iron operations in Cumberland such as the Unity Furnace which was located in Manville and Crabtree's Furnace which was located in Robin Hollow.

A Conway Bus from the 1920s. The Conways later had a fleet of buses that served generations of Cumberland's schoolchildren until the town went to an outside bus service some years ago. Courtesy of James Conway.

The Berkeley School Bus served the area of Berkeley. 1924 photo courtesy of Thomas Pryor.

Although America's industrial revolution began when Samuel Slater joined the Pawtucket cotton textile firm of Almy and Brown in 1790, the country's second cotton mill was located in Cumberland on the banks of the Abbott Run near Robin Hollow. In 1807 Elisha Waterman had built a mill on the site of an old marble plant. The mill continued under the management of several different people until the mid 1830s when it was demolished.

In 1852 Amasa Whipple, one of the partners in the original mill with Elisha Waterman, bought out his partners and constructed a new mill on the west side of the run opposite the site of the old cotton mill. Fire destroyed this mill in 1857 and it was immediately rebuilt on the same site. The new mill contained about a thousand spindles and, in the tradition of Samuel Slater, manufactured not cloth but thread to make the cloth. The original mill and its successors constituted the second cotton mill in North America thus reserving Cumberland's place in the nation's industrial history.

Mills of different types have existed in Cumberland. Some were larger than others but each played its own role in the development in the Town of Cumberland. On the west side of Diamond Hill near the northern branch of the west side of the Abbott Run is a small area known as Grant's Mill. The Tower family ran a nail factory and sawmill there before the American Revolution. The nail business utilized iron which was produced at the local blast furnaces. The sawmill was situated a few rods south of the nail factory. Joseph Brown subsequently owned and operated the property before selling it to Samuel Grant. A flood later destroyed the mill, which stood where Diamond Hill Road intersects with Pine Swamp Road, and the property remained deserted until 1818 when Joseph Grant built a new saw and grist mill in the area just north of the old mill site.

The Arnold Mills Reservoir was built in 1927 to add water to the adjacent (and older) Diamond Hill Reservoir. Somewhere under the Arnold Mills Reservoir is an area known as Tingley's Mills. Job Hathaway had operated a sawmill there until it was torn down in 1863. A gristmill was also located in the same general area. The gristmill changed hands several times until John Arnold pur-chased it about 1870.

This photo was taken in the early 1930s at the Diamond Hill Reservoir. Courtesy of Henry Klos.

A sawmill was also located in the Arnold Mills area until 1863 when it became a carriage shop which was torn down in the mid 1960s for the construction of a new road now named Nate Whipple Highway. A larger mill in the area constructed in 1825 was in existence until 1987 when it was destroyed by fire. This mill had been a machine shop owned and operated by Joseph and Ebenezer Metcalf. The brothers had been well known in their time for producing machinery and spinning frames for cotton goods. Around the 1850s the building was utilized for the production of straw, some of which must have been used in the local cottage industry of hat making. The Metcalf Mill had passed through the hands of the MacKenzie Family of Arnold Mills to Nathan W. Whipple, Jr., for whom the main road which runs through the village was named.

In 1790 Alexander Thompson moved to Cumberland from Providence. He brought with him a new industry to the town: boat building. By 1815 boat building had found its place in the northern end of the town in the village of Arnold Mills with no fewer than nineteen shops dedicated to the marine trades. The

The MacKenzie Blacksmith Shop in Arnold Mills was photographed around 1910. Postcard courtesy of Jane Wood.

principal products of these shops were yawls, surf, and whale boats. Until 1860 when the market diminished, the shops of Cumberland had created boats that were sold in Warren, Providence, and Boston.

Peck's Mill was a small yarn spinning operation. It began operation about 1810. Run by Levi Peck, its site was near the northern terminus of the area of Old Mendon Road. The stream which flows underneath the new Mendon Road, entering the Blackstone River a short distance away, did not provide sufficient water power to operate the mill and it was subsequently abandoned. The building later became a sawmill.

The Ashton Mill, built in 1867 by the Lonsdale Company, was on land that was formerly part of the Amos Ballou estate. The mill and its local residents had the modern advantage of gas lighting. The gas for these conveniences was manufactured by the Lonsdale Company and piped into Ashton. Also located in Ashton was the so-called Sinking Fund Mill so named for the great amounts of monies that were "sunk" into it. The mill contained thirty looms for the weaving of cotton cloth.

Even before the dawn of the American Industrial Revolution, the textile industry had begun to take root in the area of town known as Happy Hollow. Its name is said to have come from the fact that, in the early days of manufacturing, before the town had peace officers, the mill workers would become quite boisterous in their non-working hours. The selectmen of the town reputedly ordered them to be confined in one local building where they could sing and howl all evening long if they so desired. This, of course, made the night less than pleasant for the other local residents. However, their escapades gave the area its name: "Happy Hollow." In Happy Hollow, a small cotton factory was started in 1818 by Crawford Titus. The mill was expanded several times but eventually discontinued its operation. As the town's growth demanded newer and better constructed roads, the mill was demolished.

Oliver Chace, a pioneer cotton manufacturer, purchased mill property in Valley Falls and leased it to his sons, Harvey

Fire destroyed the last remaining mill at Arnold Mills in 1987. It had been an excellent example of early mill architecture. 1985 photo by David Balfour.

Built on the Blackstone River, the Ashton Mill is shown here in the 1920s. The owners provided housing, schools, and stores for the workers. Postcard courtesy of the Angell family.

The Old Stone Mill in Ashton from a 1920s postcard. Postcard courtesy of the Angell family.

and Samuel B. Chace. They organized the Valley Falls Company upon their father's death in 1852. In 1856 Harvey and Samuel B. Chace bought mill property located in Albion. In the 1890s the property was transferred to the Valley Falls Company in exchange for another plant located in the Valley Falls area of Cumberland. This company had been owned by a different branch of the Chace family.

Robin Hollow Mill in 1944.
Photo courtesy of James Wright.

The Rhode Island Horseshoe Company was located in Valley Falls. It began in the capital city of Providence under the name of the Union Horseshoe Company, relocating to Cumberland in 1872 and specializing in the manufacture of horseshoes and muleshoes. However, it also made iron and steel bars from scrap iron, manufactured and repaired its own machines, and maintained a copper shop. The advent of the electric trolley and the automobile brought about the eventual demise of the Rhode Island Horseshoe Company.

Modern geologists believe that there is no other town in New England richer in mineral production than Cumberland. The site of Diamond Hill was the scene of intense exploration. The search for gold led to a mine being located near Bear Hill. In June of 1904 the Bear Hill Gold Mining Company was incorporated by Daniel H. Curran, George A. Curran, and Robert A. Curran. Shares in the company cost three dollars in 1925. The company surrendered its charter in 1935 for the gold had proven to be merely iron pyrite. Lead and silver were once mined on Staples Road and old records refer to a lost silver mine located in the woods off Tower Hill Road. In the Staples Road area, a soapstone mine produced furnace linings

for the industry in Providence at the close of the nineteenth century. Copper was mined on Copper Mine Hill off Staples Road. At least fifty holes have been mined in the hill which cost an estimated half million dollars in unprofitable mining for copper ore. Tower Hill also reveals the remnants of a once flourishing copper industry.

In 1797 Benjamin Walcott operated a mill for the purpose of sawing marble at Robin Hollow. Quarry stone was available in the Berkeley area as well as Diamond Hill where the granite was reputed to be among the finest building stone in New England. The Diamond Hill Granite Company was established in 1877 with George F. Wilson as its president. A small half- mile railroad existed from the main line at Diamond Hill to a location in the quarry itself. A forty horsepower engine hoisted the cars and operated the drills for the quarry which produced granite for use in buildings and bridges all over the country. Granite cutting mills were located at Abbott Run. Diamond Hill, named for the milky and clear crystals found in its ledge, is also heavily veined with quartz. A product known as trap rock, used in the building of roads, was also quarried in Diamond Hill.

Iron Mine Hill on Elder Ballou Meeting House Road produced a relatively pure iron ore which was used in foundries in the area for many years. During the Revolution, Oziel Wilkinson and his five sons manufactured anchors, screws, farming implements, and other cast iron and wrought iron ware in Cumberland. Wilkinson made the first wing gudgeon in the colonies.

The first coal in the area was found by Timothy Dexter in 1807 while he was digging a well. In 1812 the General Assembly granted a lottery of $12,000 for the purpose of searching for coal in Cumberland. As the nineteenth century progressed, Valley Falls enjoyed a reputation as an area rich in coal. Several companies were founded over the years but none produced a burnable quality of coal. Finally, a more successful coal mining operation was established around 1840 when C. N. Clark and J. L. Clark formed the Blackstone Mining Company. The company produced about a hundred barrels per week of a fine grade burnable coal.

The Diamond Hill area is shown around 1898. Two villages surrounded the area which would later become a ski facility. Photo courtesy of Eleanor Preston.

The granite quarry in Diamond Hill circa 1890. Photo courtesy of Eleanor Preston.

Granite cut from Diamond Hill went to homes, buildings, parks, and cemeteries throughout the New England area. Photo courtesy of Eleanor Preston.

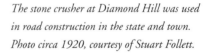

The stone crusher at Diamond Hill was used in road construction in the state and town. Photo circa 1920, courtesy of Stuart Follett.

THE BLACKSTONE CANAL

The village of Ashton is the approximate half-way point between the cities of Providence and Worcester. A so-called half-way house, or hotel, was located at the top of Store Hill and Mendon Road in the village. The leaders of Cumberland hoped to be important in the link of the two much larger cities because of the towns close proximity to the river which connected them and as early as 1796 there was discussion of a project to connect Providence and Worcester by means of a canal. Under the direction of John Brown of Providence, surveyors plotted a route and the General Assembly of Rhode Island issued a charter. However, the state of Massachusetts refused to cooperate and the project was abandoned for a time.

Old Diamond Hill Road in the 1890s reflects the serenity of village life. Photo courtesy of Eleanor Johnson.

Broad Street in Valley Falls looking south around the turn of the century. Postcard courtesy of Darlene M. and Edmond H. Guerin, Jr.

Broad Street in Valley Falls looking north around 1900. Postcard courtesy of Darlene M. and Edmond H. Guerin, Jr.

In 1882 interested parties in Providence and Worcester again discussed the subject of a canal. Massachusetts granted a charter for its construction in March of 1823, the state of Rhode Island granted a charter in June of 1823, and work began on the canal in 1824. Five commissioners undertook to oversee construction—Edward Carrington, Moses B. Ives, and Stephen Smith from Rhode Island, and Commissioners John W. Lincoln and Sylvanus Holbrook represented Massachusetts. The cost of the canal was $700,000. It was determined that $500,000 of that money was to be raised in Rhode Island and the rest would be raised in Massachusetts. Enthusiatic citizens purchased most of the stock immediately, especially in Rhode Island. Complaints from the residents of Worcester arose because of the limited amount of stock available to them. However, not unlike many enterprises of a later day, the

Boys fish at the Ashton Pond in this 1920 photo by Robert Rowbottom. Courtesy of Kenneth Rowbottom.

A Cumberland scene. Postcard courtesy of Darlene M. and Edmond H. Guerin, Jr.

Blackstone Canal was no bonanza for its stockholders.

The inaugural trip by the canal boat *Lady Carrington* began in Providence on July 1, 1828. The first boat to reach Worcester arrived on October 6, 1828. Although the Blackstone River was improved in many places as it portaged around the canal, the canal was not a financial success. Oftentimes low water prevented boats from entering the canal locks and this caused great delays. During some years, ice closed the canal for four to five months, again causing problems.

No stock dividends were ever paid to the canals' stockholders. The last toll for the passage of boats was paid on November 9,1848. The construction of the feeders and reservoirs to create the canal, however, increased the volume of water on the river which was subsequently utilized by local manufacturers along the Blackstone River.

CUMBERLAND'S MONASTERY
AND NINE MEN'S MISERY

It was in 1900 when the Most Rev. Matthew Harkins, the Roman Catholic Bishop of Providence, permitted a small group of Cistercian monks from the Society of Petit Clairvaux to relocate to a three-hundred-acre tract of land on Diamond Hill Road in Cumberland. The monks had lost their prior monastery in Nova Scotia to fire in 1899. It was to a barren, stoney property to which a group of twelve monks came with their livestock and meager possessions. Their first home was a small cabin-like building on the land, which now houses the Edward J. Hayden Library, the public library for the Town of Cumberland.

By 1902, using granite quarried on the property, the monks had constructed the front wing of a permanent abbey. The building remained their home for twenty-five years, by which time expansion was necessary for their growing numbers. Between 1922 and 1928, a beautiful church was constructed, and entitled "Our Lady of the Valley" for the beautiful Blackstone Valley, which it overlooked. Construction of other buildings continued into the 1930s. The Porter's Lodge, often referred to as the Gatehouse, was constructed in 1938.

The monks supported themselves by growing fruit and by raising dairy cattle and poultry on the surrounding lands. Within the monastery walls, they founded the Holy Rood Guild, a manufacturer of liturgical vestments for many denominations, which is still in existence.

Disaster struck on March 21, 1950, when fire destroyed the original front wing of the monastery and damaged the beautiful church to a point where it had to be destroyed. The Chapter wing, built in 1930, was also damaged. At the time of the fire, the monks had already purchased

The Abbey of Our Lady of the Valley was the centerpiece of the monastery in Cumberland. 1900 postcard courtesy of Darlene M. and Edmond H. Guerin, Jr.

After leaving their original home in Nova Scotia, the Cistercians built the monastery in Cumberland of native granite 1909 postcard courtesy of Darlene M. and Edmond H. Guerin, Jr.

(Right and opposite page, bottom) Aerial views of Our Lady of the Valley in Cumberland show the extent of the land and beauty of the buildings which the monks created. Photo courtesy of Darlene M. and Edmond H. Guerin, Jr., and postcard circa 1910, courtesy of Gordon Carr.

property in Spencer, Massachusetts, where they now reside at Saint Joseph's Abbey. For several years after the fire, the existing buildings were used as a juniorate for the Franciscan Friars of the Atonement from Graymoor, New York. After they left the area, the town took title to the property and the lands around it for recreational purposes and in 1975 located its library there. The Cumberland town administrator who supervised the purchase was Edward J. Hayden, for whom the library ultimately was named.

On the monastery grounds stands a simple stone monument—one which has honored war veterans since the year 1676. It is known as "Nine Men's Misery" and is located deep in the Cumberland woods behind the library.

Sometime during the morning of March 26, 1676, a group of Native American's ambushed a scouting party of colonial soldiers under the command of Captain Michael Pierce of Scituate, Massachusetts, in the general area of what is now the

Donald W. Wyatt Detention Facility in Central Falls, Rhode Island. Pierce's party had been reconnoitering the area of the Blackstone River when attacked. A small group escaped and fled to their garrison, a few miles away at Rehoboth (the present site of Rumford, Rhode Island). Nine soldiers retreated in the opposite direction and were pursued into Cumberland.

March 26 was a Sunday morning. When the message of the attack reached Rehoboth, the entire community was attending church services and could not be immediately disturbed. By the time the reinforcements reached the area, Pierce and

A 1950 fire devastated the monastery. Ironically, a fire truck was found in disrepair on the property, which the monks had intended to repair and use. Photo circa 1940, from the Cumberland Public Library.

The loss of this beautiful chapel was devastating to the town as well as to the Cistercian monks who resided there. They have since relocated to Spencer, Massachusetts. Postcard circa 1908, from the collection of the Cumberland Public Library.

The Town of Cumberland acquired the Cistercian Abbey for use as its public library. Postcard circa 1908, courtesy of Darlene M. and Edmond H. Guerin, Jr.

The grotto of Our Lady of the Valley Monastery shows the beautiful property which the monks maintained. Postcard from the collection of Cumberland Public Library.

his party of eight had been surrounded and massacred. Arriving too late to save them, all the soldiers could do was to bury Pierce and his men on the site and construct a stone cairn to mark their grave. The land later became the Waterman Farm. Records indicate that the spot continued to be marked by those stones over the next centuries. Indeed, when the Cistercian monks took title to the land in 1900, their resting place remained undisturbed. The State of Rhode Island, in 1928, reinforced the crude stones and placed a bronze marker on the site. The inscription on the monument reads:

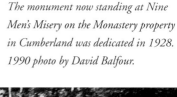

A 1908 postcard shows the stone cairn at Nine Men's Misery. From the collection of the Cumberland Public Library.

NINE MEN'S MISERY

On this spot, where they were slain by the Indians, were buried the nine soldiers captured in Pierce's Fight, March 26, 1676. Erected by the State of Rhode Island 1928.

In 1993, as fulfillment of the requirement for the status of Eagle Scout, Cumberland resident Ryan Billington marked a walking trail to the cairn and created a descriptive brochure about the monument, one of America's first honoring its soldiers.

The monument now standing at Nine Men's Misery on the Monastery property in Cumberland was dedicated in 1928. 1990 photo by David Balfour.

*This store stood at Manville and Mendon
Road around 1900 in the village of
Cumberland Hill. Courtesy of Arthur Colwell.*

PART II

The Villages of Cumberland

The different land areas of Cumberland have been known by many names over the years, names which stimulate curiosity about their origins. Many of the other areas in the town have received their names from the local home builders or the people who lived in the area (such as Lippitt Estates being named for its famous resident, former U.S. Senator Henry Lippitt). Monastery Heights was named for its proximity to the site of the Cistercian Monastery on Diamond Hill Road. Sleepy Hollow received its name from a small hotel on Sneech Pond Road. Robin Hollow was named because of the large preponderance of the red breasted birds which populate the area in spring and summer. Tower Hill in the northern part of town was named for the Tower family, early settlers in the area. Happy Hollow received its name because of its reputation of the local boisterous residents. One area known as the Village at Woonsocket Falls separated from Cumberland in 1888 and soon became a major Rhode Island city, Woonsocket.

One of the most interesting discussions about the origin of the names of the areas in Cumberland is that concerning Abbott Run. It has several stories explaining its name including one that a man named Abbott was chased by unfriendly natives in the area as residents called after him, "Run, Abbott, run!" Others claim that William Blackstone had a servant named Abbott and that the land in the area of the river which ran through the town was named for him. However, the most likely explanation is that the river rises from a swamp in land originally owned by a Mr. Abbott, and the river that ran through the land would logically be called "Abbott's Run."

THE VILLAGE OF CUMBERLAND HILL

Before the present town hall was built in Valley Falls in 1894, the village of Cumberland Hill was the seat of town government. Arguments would arise frequently as to whose home would be honored by holding the town meeting. Town meeting places were then selected by lot until the seat of government was changed to Valley Falls. The village of Cumberland Hill overlooks the Blackstone River from a lofty position high above the village of Manville (in Lincoln). The Manville Mill itself, however, was located in Cumberland; and the village provided a tavern, a store, two churches, and the only bank in town.

The Cumberland Bank (later called the Cumberland National Bank) was begun in 1823 at the stately home of Captain Amos Cook located at what is now the junction of Mendon Road and Manville Hill Road. The Cook family resided in the bank as bank officials and caretakers. The bank was chartered by the state to print notes with the bank's name on it which could be used as currency, some of which are still extant.

The Cumberland Bank continued operating until June 5, 1885. After the Panic of 1874, the bank had never fully recovered its assets and went into voluntary liquidation. The bank was the third national bank to close in the state of Rhode Island. The bank remained the home of

The family of John McLaughlin, Sr., is shown in 1912 standing in front of the former hotel property, Highland House, now called Marie Manor, in the village of Cumberland Hill. Courtesy of John McLaughlin.

the cashier, George Cook, and his family until 1929 when it became the property of Ruth Thayer. Miss Thayer was the last person to live in this graceful, columned, two-story edifice. In December of 1967, the pastor of St. Joan of Arc Roman Catholic Church had the building demolished.

It may come as a surprise to some that more than a century before Rhode Island came into its own as a tourist destination, there was a resort hotel in Cumberland Hill. Highland House, now an office building called Marie Manor and owned by the McLaughlin family, was an area hotel and boardinghouse constructed in 1843. The building was constructed by Francis Brown who served as president of the Cumberland Town Council and later was a representative to the Rhode Island General Assembly. Highland House offered guests a carriage ride up Manville Hill Road from the railroad station located there. Guests would stay in the hotel or, if they desired the outdoor life, could go camping on the shore of nearby Sneech Pond.

At the turn of the twentieth century, Sneech Pond was the location of area recreation, boating, dancing, and band concerts. A pavilion featured shore dinners in the great Rhode Island tradition. The area was served by electric streetcars and known as "Sneechaconnet Park." Earl Burlingame operated the amusement park and dance hall, but in 1929 Sneech Pond became part of the town's water supply which brought about the end of Sneech Pond as a recreation facility.

The village of Cumberland Hill was noted for its Baptist Church, built around 1795, as well as for the Cumberland Academy Company, which served the area's children as a school until the public schools were erected in the area. The Academy also housed a community library, the town's first recorded library founded in 1819. A Masonic Temple, Morning Star Lodge No. 13, F&AM, was founded

The Cook Hotel and Baptist Church in Cumberland Hill, shown around 1900, no longer stand. Courtesy of Arthur Colwell.

in Cumberland Hill in 1810, meeting first in the school and later in its temple until 1848. The Lodge now continues in the city of Woonsocket. None of these buildings are currently in existence. Many years ago, Cumberland Hill was known as "Dog Hill," so called for a tall tale of a local farmer's vicious dog.

St. Mary's Russian Orthodox Church, dedicated on September 3, 1908, was the first Eastern Orthodox Church in the state of Rhode Island. The church had received its charter in 1907. Now known as the Dormition of the Virgin Mary Orthodox Church, the one-and-a-half-story brick, Greek Athonite, monastic style building is located off Manville Hill Road. Many of the church's original parishioners worked in the Manville Mill. The church's founder, Archpriest Alexander Hotovitzky, was acknowledged a saint in the Orthodox Churches in America and Russia in 1994. Father Hotovitzky , upon his return to his native Russia, was sentenced to exile for giving religious instruction to children and preaching. He perished in a labor camp on the Solovetzky Islands in the North Sea. A commemorative mass was held in Cumberland to celebrate his canonization. The original bells of the church still peal during church services.

St. Mary's Russian Orthodox Church, now the Dormition of the Virgin Mary Orthodox Church, in a 1940 postcard. Courtesy of James Conway.

The parish of St. Joan of Arc Roman Catholic Church was established in 1929. However, the chapel, which housed the original St. Joan's Church, had been St. Mary's Chapel, an Episcopal church owned by Caroline Brown Weeden. She had erected the chapel on land granted to the Rhode Island Episcopal Church by Sally Brown, widow of Fenner Brown. Caroline

The original church of St. Joan of Arc Roman Catholic Church in Cumberland Hill was photographed in 1957. The church was destroyed in 1960 when the present church was dedicated. Courtesy of James Conway.

Brown Weeden later deeded it to her Irish (and Roman Catholic) housekeeper from whom the Roman Church obtained it. The Episcopal parish flourished until the turn of the century. At that time, the Bishop of Providence, Most Rev. Matthew Harkins, purchased the building as a Roman Catholic place of worship. The chapel at first became a mission parish to St. Joseph's Church in Ashton. In 1929 the parish was large enough to be on its own and was called St. Joan of Arc in honor of St. Joan who was canonized in May of 1920. In 1960 the present St. Joan of Arc Church was constructed and dedicated and the old chapel was demolished.

It was on Mount Pleasant View Avenue in Cumberland Hill, that one of the few major disasters associated with the town occurred. A gas explosion totally destroyed a house and took the lives of several people in 1924. Newspaper accounts tell of severe fire and of residents trapped in flaming debris.

On Mendon Road in Cumberland Hill, Ornando R. Vose built a farm house and later a Queen Anne style home. Vose was one of the area's most prominent residents, involved in real estate. Later his family started the Vose Hardware and Vose Florist businesses. Both homes date from around 1888 and 1890. Ornando Vose donated the land upon which the original Cumberland Hill School was built in 1902 at the

The Elmer Vose House in Cumberland Hill from a photo around 1910. Courtesy of Arthur Colwell.

corner of Mendon and West Wrentham Roads. It replaced a school on the site which dated from 1861. Long since boarded up, the school was originally constructed as a one-story frame building. In 1914 the original building was raised and a two story brick and wood structure was constructed on the same lot. Another former school in the area is the Edgemere School, an elementary school which contained four classrooms and was constructed in 1926 and razed; both schools were closed in the 1970s. The present Cumberland Hill School on Manville Hill Road was dedicated in the fall of 1954.

Another impressive house in Cumberland Hill is the Dexter Clark House. Built in 1862–63, the house is on the lot formerly known as the "Barney Lot" purchased from Amos Cook by Dexter Clark. Dexter Clark was both a member of the

The henhouse at the Dexter Clark house in 1910. Courtesy of the Fleurant family.

Rhode Island Senate and the Rhode Island House of Representatives. For a time he owned a grocery business in Diamond Hill and subsequently operated a gristmill and lumber yard in Woon-socket. The three-story, mansard roof, late Victorian House remains today in much the same condition as when it was built. Dexter Clark's only son sold the property in 1926 to the Girard family who later raised approximately 10,000 chickens on the property. The deed was subsequently passed to the Fleurant family who held the property until 1989. Since 1994 the property has been owned by the Woika family, and at this time is for sale.

The Dexter Clark house on Mendon Road, shown here in 1910, is an excellent example of late Victorian architecture. Photo courtesy of the Fleurant family.

THE MANVILLE MILL

Although the village of Manville is located in Lincoln, the mill for which it was named was located on the Cumberland side of the Blackstone River in the village of Cumberland Hill. The area had been involved in the business of manufacturing since before the American Revolution. The area known as Unity Village boasted a sawmill, gristmill, foundry, and blast furnace. The Lapham and Bartlett families operated the old mills and the blast furnace. The mills stood until the first of the textile mills began to be developed in the village.

In 1812, less than twenty years from the establishment of Samuel Slater's mill at Pawtucket, the Unity Cotton Manufacturing Company erected a mill at a place called the old Unity Furnace site. The Unity Furnace had utilized ore from Iron Mine Hill in Cumberland, manufacturing farm implements and cannon balls for military use. From this sprang what was to become the largest mill under one roof in the world at that time.

In 1821 control of the Unity Mill passed to the firm of Jenkins and Mann, which was largely controlled by the Mann family. The name of Unity Village was then changed to Manville. Mill number two was erected in 1826. In 1854 the Valley Falls Company, owner of the Albion Mill located a few miles downstream, purchased the entire property to protect its water rights. In 1863 new interests, calling themselves the Manville Company, purchased the property and built mill number three. It contained equipment for spinning yarn, weaving, and finishing cloth. In the 1920s the Manville Mill merged with the Jenkes Spinning Company of Pawtucket, becoming the Manville-Jenkes Company, a major textile manufacturer.

Housing for millworkers was located on both sides of the river. The boardinghouse for single and itinerant workers was

The Manville Mill in its day provided jobs for much of the Lincoln Village of Manville and the Cumberland Village of Cumberland Hill. A fire destroyed the mill in March 1957. Photo courtesy of Dea MacKinnon.

located in what later became known as the "Epheta House," a Roman Catholic Retreat House. (It has since been demolished.) Most of the worker housing associated with the mill still stands in the Town of Lincoln where tenement houses built by independent contractors dominate the area. On the Cumberland side, English style mill row houses still exist on Boyle Avenue and Mount Pleasant View Avenue.

The gas station at the corner of Manville Hill Road and Mendon Road in the late 1920s. Courtesy of Arthur Colwell.

At the close of World War II, Rhode Island's once booming textile industry departed for the south. The giant textile mills, including the Manville Mill, were left deserted and fell into disrepair. In the spring of 1955, rapid melting snow in northern New England caused the Blackstone River to overflow its banks causing major flooding all along the course of the river. Although the mill was empty, electrical power was still on and the flooding caused short circuits and electrical malfunctions resulting in an intense fire which totally destroyed the huge mill structure, the remains of which can still be seen along Flat Street.

This was the end of a major jewel in Rhode Island's industrial crown. Apartment complexes now stand where the mighty looms once hummed and the old mill bell, which called thousands of laborers to work at the Manville Mill, now stands on the lawn of Emmanuel Episcopal Church on Nate Whipple Highway.

The Conway Ice Wagon around 1910. Courtesy of James Conway, from the collection of the Conway Bus Company.

Opposite: An 1870 map of Valley Falls from the collection of Gordon Carr.

THE VILLAGE OF VALLEY FALLS

With its textile mills and its prime location along the tracks of the Providence and Worcester Railroad, Valley Falls became the logical choice to become the new seat of government in Cumberland. The Cumberland Town Hall was built in Valley Falls at the northeast corner of Broad and Mill Streets in 1894. Its construction ended the constant disputes of whose home would be the site of the town council meetings. The architectural firm of William R. Walker and Son designed the three-story, Colonial Revival style building located on land previously owned by the Valley Falls Company and in view of Valley Falls Heritage Park, recently created from the ruins of one of the old mills.

The name Town Hall actually refers to the meeting room within the building called the Town House. However, it has been common practice to use it to represent the entire structure. Some portions of the Town Hall have been restored to its original condition. Work continues to expose the original brick walls, ornate banisters, and wooden wainscoting throughout the building. Much of the actual meeting room has been lost to prior subdivision for office space. However, restoration is continuing with the hopes of recreating some of the building's original grandeur.

Seven years after he had built a mill on the banks of the Blackstone River in Pawtucket, Samuel Slater's associates Elisha Waterman and Benjamin Walcott erected a second cotton mill at Robin Hollow in Valley Falls. This mill, later known as the

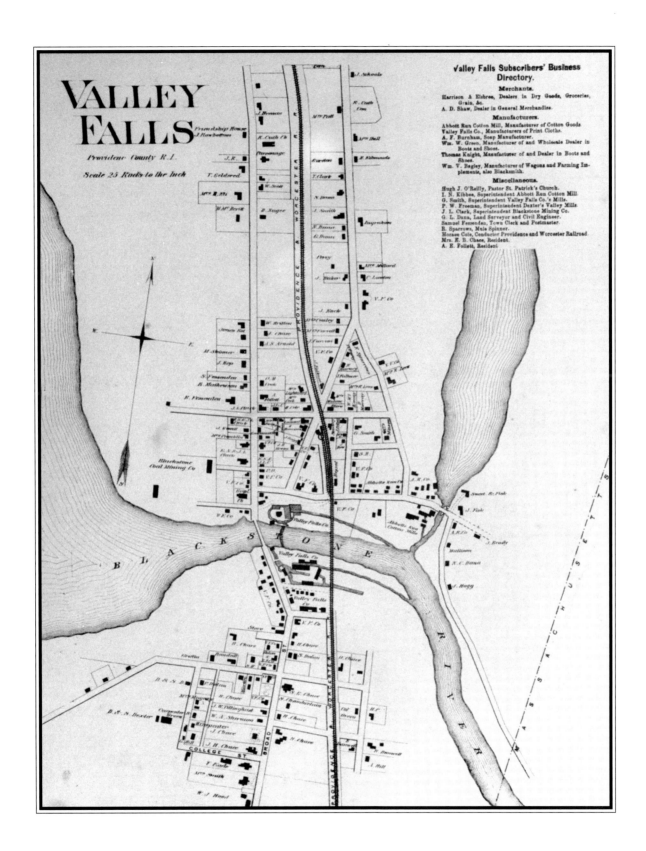

VALLEY FALLS

Providence County R.I.

Scale 25 Rods to the Inch

Friendship House
J. Hawbottines

Valley Falls Subscribers' Business Directory.

Merchants.

Harrison A Kibbee, Dealers in Dry Goods, Groceries, Grain, &c.
A. D. Shaw, Dealer in General Merchandise.

Manufacturers.

Abbott Run Cotton Mill, Manufacturer of Cotton Goods.
Valley Falls Co., Manufacturers of Print Cloths.
A. F. Burnham, Soap Manufacturer.
Wm. W. Green, Manufacturer of and Wholesale Dealer in Boots and Shoes.
Thomas Knight, Manufacturer of and Dealer in Boots and Shoes.
Wm. V. Bagley, Manufacturer of Wagons and Farming Implements, also Blacksmith.

Miscellaneous.

Hugh J. O'Reilly, Pastor St. Patrick's Church.
I. N. Kibbee, Superintendent Abbott Run Cotton Mill.
G. Smith, Superintendent Valley Falls Co.'s Mills.
P. W. Freeman, Superintendent Dexter's Valley Mills.
J. L. Clark, Superintendent Blackstone Mining Co.
G. L. Dunn, Land Surveyor and Civil Engineer.
Samuel Fessenden, Town Clerk and Postmaster.
R. Sparrows, Mule Spinner.
Horace Cole, Conductor Providence and Worcester Railroad.
Mrs. E. B. Chace, Resident.
A. E. Follett, Resident.

The Cumberland Town Hall was built in 1894 in the village of Valley Falls on property overlooking the Blackstone River and near the city of Central Falls. Postcard circa 1900, courtesy of Darlene M. and Edmond H. Guerin, Jr.

"Abbott Run Cotton Mill," was the second cotton mill in the United States. This event led the way for Cumberland's development as a textile manufacturing center in the nineteenth century. About 1818 Crawford Titus established a second factory at nearby Happy Hollow. By 1850 Valley Falls had gained a reputation as an important industrial center with large brick and stone mills lining the Blackstone River. Fire destroyed the largest of these mills in the 1930s; however, its history lives on today through the creation of Valley Falls Heritage Park on its site within the shadow of the Cumberland Town Hall.

Other industry in the village of Valley Falls included coal mining. Timothy Dexter, a Valley Falls farmer, unearthed anthracite (hard coal) on his property in 1808. Within a year, the coal mine was supplying heat for a cotton mill and a local blacksmithy. However, the story of Timothy Dexter and his coal mine is not a happy one. After two years, he shut down operations as wood for heating was still plentiful and burning coal was considered by many to be too time consuming. Within twenty years of the discovery of his mine, with local wood supplies depleted and coal being brought in from Pennsylvania, Timothy reopened his mine only to lose his son Benjamin in a mining accident. Dexter again closed his mine.

A 1907 postcard, the Valley Falls Bridge connects the village of Valley Falls to the city of Central Falls. Vintage lighting was recently placed on the bridge. Courtesy of Darlene M. and Edmond H. Guerin, Jr.

Seven years later, John Alexander and three Mason brothers took a lease on Dexter's mine. A year later Joseph Mason was killed while preparing a mine shaft. In 1837 a fire destroyed the mine company's building. Mining continued through 1840 when the mine filled with water. Captain Thomas Martin continued working the area for several more years until he too admitted defeat. Town maps at that time refer to the current Dexter Street as "Coal Mine Road" in connection with these endeavors.

The Blackstone Coal Mining Company began mining in the same general area of Valley Falls in 1848.

Upper Broad Street in Valley Falls around 1900 from a postcard. Courtesy of Darlene M. and Edmond H. Guerin, Jr.

The railroad in Valley Falls in October of 1920. The New York–New Haven Railroad was a presence in Valley Falls until the Providence and Worcester regained control of the railroad that it had originally started. Courtesy of Walter Gelinas.

John Francis Clark, secretary of the firm, later became Cumberland town clerk for a period of sixteen years. Clark's home is still standing on Broad Street in the shadow of the Cumberland Town Hall. It is an elaborate, two-and-one-half story Queen Anne style house at the corner of Broad and Titus Street and is considered unique among Cumberland's homes for its ornamentation. The house is believed to have been designed by the same firm that designed the Cumberland Town Hall, William R. Walker and Son. Clark also held several other offices in the town, including town treasurer, tax assessor, and superintendent of schools. He also served in the Rhode Island General Assembly from 1878 to 1884.

By 1908 the Blackstone Coal Mining Company had gone bankrupt. Cyrus Taft, a trustee of the firm, undertook the task of liquidating its property. Unfortunately, Taft and the other investors neglected to do what Timothy Dexter had always done—fill in the shafts. By 1984 several cave-ins were reported

Workers at the Rolling Mill Horseshoe Factory, also known as Union Horseshoe factory, pose around 1880. Courtesy of Gertrude Tuscher.

in the area formerly owned by the Blackstone Coal Mining Company.

The Rhode Island Horse Shoe Company operated in Valley Falls from 1867 until 1914. Horse shoes had previously been fashioned by local blacksmiths until the Union Horseshoe Company relocated to Cumberland from Providence and changed its name to the Rhode Island Horseshoe Company. The demise of the local horse-car system, brought about by the advent of the electric street railroad in the 1890s, lessened the demand for the product of the horse shoe company.

Rapid industrial growth prompted the construction of single and multi-unit houses, as well as institutional buildings.

By 1870 more than one hundred existed along Broad Street, High Street, and on the streets in between. Saint Patrick's Church with its cemetery on High Street, was founded in 1861 as the first Roman Catholic Church in the area. Its parishioners were originally the Irish workers of the area. The church was totally rebuilt in 1936.

The Catholic Institute of St. Patrick's Church, photographed around 1907, was constructed as a social club, library, and school. It was destroyed in 1941. Courtesy of Gordon Carr.

The creation of the Catholic Institute in 1894 provided St. Patrick's Parish with a social center contained in a huge castle-like structure on Broad Street. It was founded to promote the intellectual, physical, and spiritual well being of its members. In its beginning only men, eighteen years and older, could join. The building held two bowling alleys, billiard rooms, a library, an auditorium seating four hundred and a meeting room seating one hundred and forty. It was destroyed by fire in 1941.

Trolley tracks can be seen on the street in front of St. Patrick's Church, around 1898. This was the second Roman Catholic Church erected in the Blackstone Valley. Courtesy of Joseph Beck.

The Broad Street Bridge constructed in 1915 connects the town of Cumberland with its neighbor, the city of Central Falls.

The Town of Cumberland purchased the former Currier

The rectory at St. Patrick's Church. Postcard circa 1908, courtesy of Darlene M. and Edmond H. Guerin, Jr.

St. Patrick's Church and School from a postcard around 1907. In the 1900s, postcards were readily available showing private homes and assorted attractions in the Blackstone Valley. Courtesy of Darlene M. and Edmond H. Guerin, Jr.

It is believed that the Currier House was part of the Underground Railroad. A tunnel in the basement may have led under Broad Street to other Currier property, then existing on what is now the Town Hall's parking lot. The house was demolished in the early 1970s. From The Times.

properties that surrounded the Cumberland Town Hall. Part of the property became the parking lot adjacent to the Town Hall. Across the street was the Currier Mansion and carriage house, reputed to be a station in the Underground Railroad before the Civil War. The house was built by Andrew J. Currier, a manager for the Albion Company and the Valley Falls Company, who worked for the Chace family, owners of the two mills. The Chaces, who were Quakers, were well known for being active in the anti-slavery movement and in assisting runaway slaves to reach freedom. Andrew's daughter Carrie Currier resided in the mansion until her death on November 7, 1966. After years of neglect, the town eventually demolished the mansion and carriage house to create basketball and other assorted courts for local children's recreation.

Elizabeth Buffum Chace, daughter of abolitionist Arnold Buffum and wife to industrialist Samuel Chace, assisted in the Underground Railroad from her home in Valley Falls. Slaves were brought to Valley Falls by way of the Underground through the Massachusetts city of Fall River. Mr. and Mrs. Chace then assisted in getting them to Worcester for their trip in Canada. After the Civil War, she became a crusader for women's rights and formed, with Paulina Wright Davis, the Rhode Island Woman Suffrage Association. She served as president of the group from 1870 until 1899. Mrs. Chace also supported prison reform, a state school for orphans, and influenced the Providence City Council to require women matrons for all police stations. She worked tirelessly with Sarah Doyle to force Brown University to admit women to its classes.

THE VILLAGE OF LONSDALE

The village which Cumberland residents know as "Lonsdale" is actually a continuation of the village of Lonsdale in the Town of Lincoln, Cumberland's neighbor across the Blackstone River. No clear record exists of where the name Lonsdale actually originated. The Lonsdale Company was incorporated in 1834, succeeding the Lonsdale Water Power Company, which had its beginning in 1825. Old English records indicate that members of the Lonsdale family wrote some songs and ballads of Cumberland. It can thus be assumed that some sort of relationship with the location of Lonsdale in England might have existed.

The Lonsdale Company had earlier established a number of massive mills in Lincoln and in 1860, the company expanded its operation across the river into Cumberland. It erected a large, brick mill in that year followed by two other mills in 1871 and 1886. The 1886 mill is the edifice that today is better known as the Ann and Hope Department Store.

In building the Ann and Hope Mill, however, the company destroyed the park-like setting of William Blackstone's "Study Hill." The Lonsdale Company moved Blackstone's remains to the mill yard and in doing so further destroyed any evidence of Blackstone's life there.

The Lonsdale Company housed its workers in company owned buildings which they built. It also provided them with their school, some stores, and a church. In this way, the company supported much of their community life. During the most prosperous time, millworkers of Lonsdale enjoyed better than average living conditions, with many workers owning their own homes. The mill itself was one of the first to use the Draper loom, which had automatic bobbins. Its major products were cotton cloths and cambric muslins.

The Ann and Hope Mill was named for the China trade clipper ship, the *Ann and Hope*, built in 1798 for the prominent shipping firm of Brown and Ives. The ship's name was

The Ann and Hope Cotton Mill was photographed in 1907 for this postcard. The Lonsdale Company had erected the mill and millhouses in the surrounding area in the years between 1872 and 1886. Courtesy of Gordon Carr.

derived from the first names of the wives (Ann Carter Brown and Hope Brown Ives) of Lonsdale Company President Nicholas Brown and company Treasurer Robert Ives. The partnership of Brown and Ives proved to be a fruitful one. The Brown family donated money to the Rhode Island College which, in gratitude, changed its name to Brown University, an institution of considerable reknown today.

During the 1930s the mill closed down, and the Lonsdale Company held a liquidation sale in 1935 to dispose of its local properties. Brick duplex houses were priced at $4,830 to $5,230, six or seven rooms to each half. A block of six brick tenements sold for $2,530. During World War II, the mill became a Naval Repair Station and from June of 1943 to February of 1947, the Dahlstrom Company of Texas had a heavy equipment repair company in the mill. It survives today as the home of the first discount department store in the country, the Ann and Hope Department Store begun in Cumberland in 1953.

The Lonsdale Primitive Methodist Church, on the corner of Bowen and Broad Streets, was organized in 1887. The church building itself was dedicated in 1891 on land purchased for the church from Mr. and Mrs. Simon Mowry for the price of twelve cents per square foot. Its original organ was purchased from the Lonsdale Baptist Church, and has since been replaced. In 1914, the outside of the church was altered and Sunday School rooms were added. Renovated in 1961, the church now goes by the name Cumberland Community Methodist Church.

The William E. Blackstone School, named for a descendant of William Blackstone who donated the land for the school, was constructed in 1872 and in the style of its day contained only four classrooms. It was built by the Lonsdale Company and replaced an earlier school on the site. Since its closing in 1974 as a school, it has been converted to a medical building.

Central Grammar School was erected in 1925 containing

The Lonsdale Primitive Methodist Church, now known as the Cumberland Community Methodist Church, was dedicated in 1891. This postcard is probably from 1907. Courtesy of Darlene M. and Edmond H. Guerin, Jr.

eight classrooms. Closed in 1994 by the school department, it is now owned by the town.

The first Cumberland High School was located on the present site of the new B. F. Norton Elementary School. It had been erected in 1889, with additions in 1916 and 1931, and contained twenty classrooms. It became the B. F. Norton School when the new high school was constructed in 1961. Only one wing of the original building remains.

One of the oldest existing houses in the area is the Kent-Smith-Laxton House on Broad Street, located across from the site of William Blackstone's Study Hill. When Hezekiah Kent and his wife Lavinia (Dexter) arrived in the area, all that remained of Blackstone's large estate was a cellar hole and a few trees of his famed apple orchard. A small building on the site of the original Kent House is where Joseph Jenks Arnold began his first bakery in 1875. He later moved the bakery, and later still the building itself, to Lincoln where it be-came known as the Lonsdale bakery. The original house dates from 1795 and in 1795 the land for the house was sold to Hezekiah Kent by Isaac Draper. The descendents of Kent later sold the home to the Lonsdale Company which in turn sold it to Esther and James Smith. The grandson of this couple, Stephen Laxton, eventually became the owner of the home.

Near the Kent House stands the mansion of Dr. Lucius Fayette Clark Garvin, a local doctor who was elected governor of the state of Rhode Island and served from 1903 to 1905. Dr. Garvin was elected thirteen times to the General Assembly as Rhode Island Representative and three times as Rhode Island State Senator. Dr. Garvin was a well respected physician whose dedication was well known among the local millworkers. Former Governor Garvin, upon returning to his private

This was the home of the Rhode Island governor, Dr. Lucius Fayette Garvin (1903–1905), a long-time physician in the Lonsdale area of Cumberland. The house still exists on Broad Street and is privately owned. 1907 postcard courtesy of Darlene M. and Edmond H. Guerin, Jr.

The "Catholic Oak" was renowned from 1843 when Reverend James Cook Richmond preached beneath its boughs. This postcard from around 1908 depicts the huge tree with its protective iron fence. The first tree is long since gone although a replacement tree still exists on the site on Ann and Hope Way. Courtesy of Gordon Carr.

practice after years in political office, was known to have ridden a bicycle to visit the sick. Most of his patients could not afford his fifty cent office charge. Thus, as a cost cutting measure, he sold his horse and carriage and bought a bicycle. The tall, distinguished figure in his long white duster, hunched over the handlebars of his bicycle, became a familiar sight on the Lonsdale streets of the time.

In 1812 Isaac Wilkinson built the Valley Falls Turnpike, now called Broad Street, from the border of Pawtucket to the area known as Lonsdale (near Blackstone's grave). In this same area, the Catholic Oak was to stand, a huge oak tree under which people came to worship from all over the area, even as far away as Providence. The Rev. James Cook Richmond, an Episcopal Clergyman, first gave a sermon there in June of 1843.

It is said that Rev. Richmond went to the Kent House and posted a notice of his pending sermon. His renown as a speaker was spread by the local worshippers and the stagecoach drivers who carried people there in their liveries. It is also believed that Rev. Richmond took acorns from the oak and planted them in England while visiting that country. There, reportedly, they thrived. The Catholic Oak remained a landmark in the area for many years. Postcards from as late as 1910 show the impressive oak surrounded by a protective iron fence. However, the original oak tree perished in 1947 and was replaced by another tree. Several gavels and other objects of art were carved from the remnants of the original tree. These are now on display at the Blackstone Valley Historical Society as part of their permanent collection. Indeed, the official seal of the society includes oak leaves and acorns commemorating the Catholic Oak.

THE VILLAGE OF ARNOLD MILLS

The village of Arnold Mills, a national historic district, was once called East Cumberland. It had its origins in 1734, when permission was granted to William Walcott, Samuel Streeter, and Daniel Wilkinson to develop a mill on the site. The Furnace Carolina was erected in the area in 1735 by John Metcalf of Dedham, Massachusetts. By 1736 the blast furnace had been sold to Dr. William Clarke of Boston and a group of other prominent Boston merchants. The name under which the village is now known derives from the arrival of Amos Arnold from Smithfield who bought the sawmill and the mill privilege in 1745. He added a gristmill which provided the surrounding area with grain and corn meal. By the year 1831 the area became known as Arnolds Mills. The small village by the brook which was home to Arnold and his neighbors still stands although the industry and shops which were housed there no longer exist. The private residences on what is now called Sneech Pond Road date from the eighteenth century. Arnold's home, a one-and-one-half-story gambrel-roof house on Sneech Pond Road remains as a testimony to the village's namesake.

The Main Street in Arnold Mills, formerly known as the village of East Cumberland, is shown around 1907 in a postcard of the era. Courtesy of Gordon Carr.

In 1825 Ebenezer and Joseph Metcalf established a machine shop in the village which had also been used for grain storage, as a blacksmith shop, and as a wagon shop. It stood until 1987 when fire destroyed it, one of the last remaining mills of its kind in the state.

In 1720 the Colonial Cottage was built by Benjamin Walcott on Sneech Pond Road (now Nate Whipple Highway). Although the home might date from the late 1600s, Walcott is credited with its construction. He served in Captain Elisha Waterman's Minutemen Company during the American Revolution and was also a member of a local committee to

The Colonial Cottage, also known as the Walcott Homestead, dates from 1720 but could be older. This photo dates from 1898 as indicated by the stars in American flag. The house is one of many well-preserved colonial homes in Arnold Mills, site of the Arnold Mills Fourth of July Parade. Photo courtesy of Lee Allison.

provide assistance to the families of absent soldiers during the same war. His son Benjamin S. Walcott later owned weaving mills at Abbott Run. Another son, John, ran the general store and a mill in Arnold Mills. John later lived with his family in the Colonial Cottage which is frequently called the Captain John Walcott House (he was a captain in the Cumberland militia) in his memory. The house is a two-and-one-half-story Colonial with a large brick center chimney. The old Fog Mill, which had manufactured wrought-iron nails, was located behind the house.

The village of Arnold Mills is dissected by the Nate Whipple Highway, constructed in 1963 to replace the rambling Sneech Pond Road. The new road was named for local fire chief Nathan W. Whipple, Jr. To make way for the new road, the Carriage Repository was destroyed. Part of the original

Even the animals got into the picture, including these pets of the owners of the Colonial Cottage in 1898. These photos are well preserved remnants of a quieter time in Cumberland's history. Photo courtesy of Lee Allison.

Sneech Pond Road, which now parallels the new highway, is the site of seven homes which contribute to the Arnold Mills National Historic District. The Arnold Mills Bridge on Sneech Pond Road, constructed in 1886, is one of at least six bridges in Cumberland built by the Boston Bridge Works.

The Abbott Run flows through Arnold Mills from the Diamond Hill and Arnold Mills Reservoirs. Today, some of the surrounding houses in the area remain on land leased to their owners by the Pawtucket Water Authority which owns the reservoirs.

The Arnold Mills Methodist Church was dedicated in 1827 and open to all denominations. It 1832 it became a Methodist meetinghouse. The former Arnold Mills Freight Station (built circa 1877) still stands where it was moved in 1933. Two historical cemeteries border the church property. Arnold Mills Methodist Pastor Rev. Horatio Crawford is credited with founding the July Fourth Arnold Mills Parade in 1927. The first parade is believed to have taken place after massive bonfires burnt the remaining buildings on the site of the Arnold Mills Reservoir on July 3, 1927.

The Cumberland Detective Society, formed shortly after the incorporation of the town to discourage theft, held annual clambakes in the Arnold Mills area for many years. Known as the "Horse Thief Society" until the advent of the automobile, it disbanded in 1930 and donated its clambake equipment to the North Cumberland Fire Department. The fire department took over the planning of the Arnold Mills

Arnold Mills Methodist Church was created for the worship of all denominations in 1827. It became a Methodist meetinghouse in 1832. Minor alterations throughout the years have made this building an outstanding example of new England religious architecture. 1909 postcard courtesy of Darlene M. and Edmond H. Guerin, Jr.

The Methodist Parsonage is on the grounds of the Arnold Mills Methodist Church. 1910 postcard courtesy of Jane Wood.

A carriage repair shop was located in the Arnold Mills area. Photo circa 1910, courtesy of Eva Schofield.

Parade in 1931 as a means of raising funds for the department and continued the clambakes of the old Detective Society. In 1964 transfer of the Arnold Mills Parade went to the Arnold Mills Parade Association founded by H. "Hank" Seymour Wiley, a parade participant since 1951. The Arnold Mills Parade Association proudly continues the tradition of organizing the annual July Fourth parade, road race, and "Concert on the Green" (on the grounds of the Arnold Mills Methodist Church).

The Arnold Mills Parade on the Fourth of July has been an annual event since 1927. From its origins as an Ancient and Horribles parade, it has grown to be a three division parade highlighted by antique and custom autos and tractors as seen in this photo from the 1976 parade celebrating the America's Bicentennial. Photo courtesy of Lou DeFusco.

The Arnold Mills Schoolhouse was constructed about 1828 and housed students in its one room until it was replaced by the Community School in 1924. The schoolhouse building then served as the North Cumberland Fire

Department until its new fire station was built in 1946. The fire department has named the station "Whipple Station" in honor of longtime fire chief, Nathan W. Whipple, Jr.

The Cumberland Grange No. 2 was the first grange organized in northern Rhode Island in 1888. Built in 1895, the building itself is located next to the present Community School. Edwin F. Carpenter, a Grange member, donated the land for its construction. A nearby shelter was created to accommodate twenty horses, used by the members to travel to meetings. The first agricultural newspaper in America was the *American Farmer* begun in Cumberland in 1777. The Cumberland Grange published a newspaper called *The Gleaner* which was published monthly from 1899 until December of 1907. Dwindling membership caused the building to be sold

The Arnold Mills Schoolhouse on October 8, 1908. Schools in this era, before the establishment of a townwide school system, were one-room district schools having students of many ages in many grades. Photo courtesy of Elizabeth Allen.

The Cumberland Grange No. 2, as seen in a 1912 postcard. Courtesy of Doris Palmer.

when the Cumberland Grange relinquished its charter. The building is now a private home.

The Former Friends Meeting House/Arnold Mills Community House, located on the corner of Abbott Run Valley Road and Hillside Drive, was originally constructed as a Quaker meetinghouse. It was used as such from 1809 to 1926. In 1942 it became the Arnold Mills Community House and for a time housed the Arnold Mills Library until the local village libraries were consolidated at the Cumberland Monastery property in 1975. The library wing was donated by Miss Margaret Stearns, a local benefactress of the Arnold Mills community.

THE VILLAGE OF ASHTON

Built above the flood plains of the Blackstone River, the

The Quaker Meeting House, now known as Arnold Mills Community House, also served as the local branch of the town library before the construction of the Cumberland Public Library. 1907 postcard courtesy of Darlene M. and Edmond H. Guerin, Jr.

village of Ashton was probably named for the English town of Ashton-Under-Lyne. Levi Peck operated a small yarn spinning operation in the area about 1810, but water power in the area was not sufficient to run this mill successfully. As the textile industry began to dominate the economy of the town, this village sprung up in 1863. This was when the Lonsdale Company purchased an area near the hill overlooking the river from the Amos Ballou estate and erected a huge textile mill there powered by both water and steam.

The company built many brick English style mill houses for its workers, a mill operated school, and a company store. In 1867 the Lonsdale Company reinterred the contents of the graves of a former cemetery on its property to the cemetery at the corner of Scott Road and Mendon Road.

The Ashton Mill's forty thousand spindles and thirty looms turned out some of America's finest cambric muslin. The mill and its employees had gas lighting provided by the company and pumped into Ashton. The company eventually closed the mill in 1935.

A 1955 flood in the village of Ashton.
Photo courtesy of Herbert Preston.

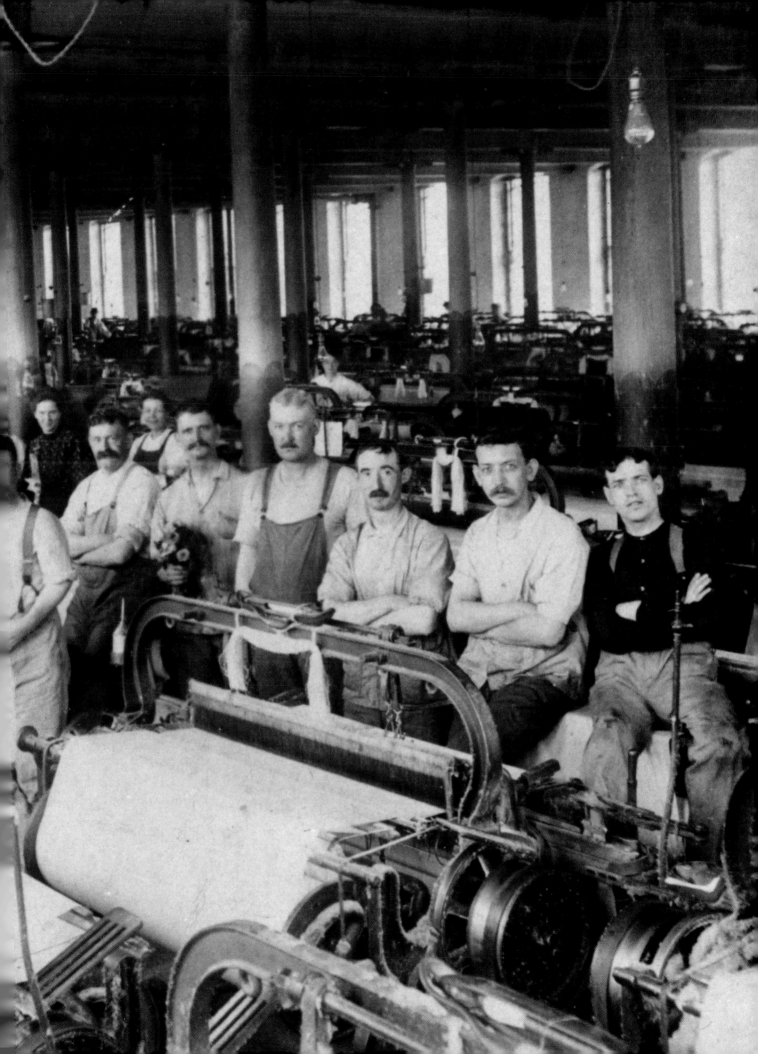

On an 1838 map, there were not many houses in the area. The Amos Ballou Tavern was located on the west side of Mendon Road near Store Hill Road. Store Hill Road is so called because A. J. Ballou's Store and Post Office were also in the general area. A sawmill in the village was operated by a Mr. L. Streeter at that time. In a map of 1870 a chapel known as St. John's was located where the St. John's Episcopal parish house is now. In 1868 the cornerstone of the present St. John's Church was laid.

The Wilkinson family of Ashton were great inventors. Jeremiah Wilkinson planted the first cherry orchard in the area off Angell Road giving Jeremiah's nickname, "Cherry."

A view of Ashton Mills from the George Washington Bridge that connects the Town of Cumberland to the Town of Lincoln. Mills sprang up on the Blackstone River in every city and town in the Blackstone Valley. Courtesy of Jean Schofield Madden.

An old mill in Ashton. Postcard circa 1908, courtesy of Joseph E. Coduri.

Jeremiah's son Jeremiah was an extremely talented iron worker. Born in 1741 he was probably the greatest creative genius of his day. He made the first silver spoons in the area, made a carding

machine for wool and was the first person to draw wire with the aid of a machine. However, he is best known for a mechanized process of cold cutting nails. Jeremiah also developed a process for making molasses from corn stalks.

Daniel Wilkinson, his son, became active in town politics. Erected in 1824, Daniel Wilkinson's house still stands on Angell Road. Jeremiah's son James invented surveying tools. Jemima Wilkinson, Jeremiah's sister, was a preacher and prophet who, at the age of twenty-three, awoke from a coma believing that her body had been taken over by a spirit. Her followers established a meetinghouse in East Greenwich before moving to western New York in 1790 where she and her followers founded the community of Pen Yan.

Jeptha Wilkinson, born in 1791 in Cumberland, is believed to have invented the revolver. Another Rhode Islander,

The Wilkinson Tavern at Bear Hill Road and Diamond Hill Road was owned and operated by the Monkhouse family, but no longer exists. Photo circa 1898, courtesy of John Bessette.

Colonel Samuel Colt, is alleged to have copied Wilkinson's design and had it patented first. Hence the revolver continues to be known as the Colt revolver. David Wilkinson invented a gauge and sliding lathe. He also is reputed to have cast the first solid cannon. The Wilkinson family was also associated with Elijah Ormsbee in his plans to construct steamboats. Nine years before Robert Fulton and his steamboat, the *Clermont*, made the history books, Elijah Ormsbee and David Wilkinson constructed a steamboat called the *Experiment* in 1792. The boat had a "goosefoot" paddle rather than a sidewheel. The partnership of Ormsbee and Wilkinson was abandoned so the planned steamboat rides between Newport and Providence never materialized. Robert Fulton therefore received credit for the creation of the steamboat.

The Lippitt Estate was the summer home of Henry F. Lippitt. The large brick Colonial Revival house was constructed on approximately four hundred acres off Angell Road around 1910. Henry F. Lippitt was a mill owner in nearby Woonsocket who later served a term as governor of the State of Rhode Island (1875–1877). The house itself was destroyed by fire twice. The area later became a summer resort area before becoming a subdivision in the middle 1900s.

Near the former Lippitt Estate is the house known as "Grayrock" which is visible from Interstate 295. Constructed in 1920, probably from granite quarried at a local site, the house stands on the cherry orchard formerly owned by the Wilkinson family. It was built by Squire Senior Nicholson, president and treasurer of the Nicholson/Thackray Company, a grocery chain which

The summer residence of former Governor (1875–1877) Henry F. Lippitt stood in the area now referred to as Lippitt Estates off Angell Road in Cumberland. Photo circa 1918, courtesy of Joseph Billington.

In 1920 fire destroyed the Lippitt Mansion which had overlooked four hundred acres owned by the former governor. Photo by Robert Rowbottom, courtesy of Kenneth Rowbottom.

later became part of The First National (Finast) chain.

In 1873 the Universalist Church built Union Chapel, later called the Four Corners Community Chapel. Sarah (Cook) Carpenter started a Sunday School in the one-room District School in the four corners area of Diamond Hill Road and Angell Road. Mrs. Carpenter, wife of George H. Carpenter, created a Ladies Circle Society which raised the money for building the church. The one-room schoolhouse became the church hall in 1926 when it was moved to its present location (attached to the church) from its original location across the street.

THE VILLAGE OF BERKELEY

Robert H. Ives of the Lonsdale Company decreed that the Berkeley Mill, built in 1872, and its surrounding village be named in honor of the Reverend George Berkeley, an eighteenth-century philosopher who lived at that time in Middletown, Rhode Island. Berkeley was an essayist and scholar whose dream was to establish an Anglican college on the beautiful island of Bermuda with Rhode Island providing its food supply. His dream was not fulfilled and he returned to Ireland and was made bishop of the church there.

The Berkeley Mill was similar in appearance to the Lonsdale Company's mills in Ashton and Lonsdale, but it differed in that it was powered by a five hundred horse power Corliss engine rather than by water power. At that time,

Joseph Billington stands in foreground of the Lippitt Mansion in 1931 after it had been rebuilt. The mansion was destroyed by fire again in 1938, after which the area became a subdivision known as Lippitt Estates. Photo courtesy of Joseph Billington.

The Chapel Four Corners church and school are shown in a 1908 postcard. Supporters have increased its size with additions and it still stands at the crossroads of Angell Road and Diamond Hill Road. Postcard courtesy of Gordon Carr.

George Corliss had the country's largest steam engine factory in the state capital of Providence. His designs earned him international fame including first prize at the Paris Exposition in 1867. His engine enabled the mill to turn out vast quantities of cambric muslin and fine shirtings.

The ethnic makeup of the village at the time was mostly English and Irish. The Berkeley Methodist Church, located on Mendon Road, was built for the employees of the mills and was the first church where Rev.

This photo of the Ashton Mill with locomotive probably dates from the early 1920s. Photo courtesy of the Angell family whose ancestors were the Wilkinsons of Ashton.

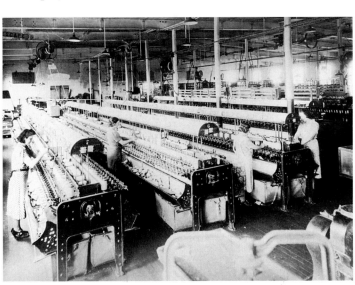

Factory workers from around 1900. The cotton and textile mills spurred the growth of the villages in Cumberland through the 1930s. Photo courtesy of Jim Acciaolli.

Mendon Road in Berkeley Village was built over a dirt road in use since colonial times. Postcard dated April 22, 1927, courtesy of Darlene M. and Edmond Guerin, Jr.

The bridges of Berkeley Village connect the village to its neighboring town of Lincoln on the other side of the Blackstone River. Postcard circa 1910, courtesy of the Angell family.

Norman Vincent Peale spoke when he was a young divinity student. The Late Victorian Carpenter Gothic Church is a one-story, end gable roof building which no longer is used as a church. Also included in the village area were a railroad passenger station and the Berkeley School. The school was constructed in 1872 with six classrooms and closed around 1981.

Berkeley Methodist Church, shown about 1908. The church has for a long time been utilized as different businesses. Postcard courtesy of Joseph E. Coduri.

The Berkeley Church, postcard circa 1900, courtesy of Darlene M. and Edmond Guerin, Jr.

The Berkeley Hall, as seen in 1908, was located on the corner of Martin Street and Mendon Road across from the Berkeley Church. The destruction of this building with its unique spires and architecture was a tremendous loss for the village. Postcard courtesy of Joseph E. Coduri.

The Berkeley School was constructed in 1872, shown here on a postcard around 1908. Closed in 1981, it is now owned by a private business. Postcard courtesy of Joseph E. Coduri.

THE VILLAGE OF DIAMOND HILL

The source of many of the capital city's curbstones and foundation stones was Cumberland's Diamond Hill. Long before Diamond Hill became a ski run and state park, the area was known for its granite quarries. The gatehouse at the Diamond Hill Reservoir was constructed from quartz from the Diamond Hill Quarry around 1884. The quarry was in operation until the middle 1930s. The area consisted of two distinct villages, located next to each other—Diamond Hill Red and Diamond Hill Blue—which housed quarry workers who cut stone and transported it by rail to a crushing apparatus. The remains of these areas are protected today on state owned land listed as the Diamond Hill Management area, opposite the Diamond Hill State Park. During World War II, buildings

Welcome to Ashton! Around the turn of the century, a person's travel itinerary to different parts of the state and country was typically announced in the local newspapers. Postcards were used as a means to keep in touch with friends and relatives. 1910 postcard courtesy of Scott Welton.

The Diamond Hill Store and Post Office on Diamond Hill Road in the village of Diamond Hill was photographed for this 1907 postcard. Courtesy of Eleanor Johnson.

were constructed there for the testing of firearms by the military and the manufacturers of the Johnson automatic rifle. An old silver mine also is in the area, long since closed.

The village was originally called Diamond Hill Plain. It boasted a hotel, an area store, and many private homes constructed by wealthy citizens originally connected to the nearby mining and iron operations. The Diamond Hill Cemetery on Reservoir Road contains the graves of many of the early settlers. The railroad not only carried granite from the area but also passengers. Indeed, schoolchildren took the train from Diamond Hill and the areas in the northern part of the town to the high school in Valley Falls until the advent of school buses. The curtailment of local passenger service made the train obsolete.

Because of its height of 481 feet, Diamond Hill ski area gained a reputation as one of New England's best. In the time before chair lifts, machine-made snow, and mass transportation to New Hampshire and Vermont, people came to Rhode Island to ski Diamond Hill. They came from New York by Colonial Line Steamboat to Providence and took a motor coach for a day on the slopes. There was a rope tow, a ski jump, and a toboggan run. Some skiers of Diamond Hill even made the United States Olympic Team.

The Diamond Hill Hotel, located in the area of the present St. John Vianney Roman Catholic Church, was also reputed to be a brothel. Postcard circa 1908, courtesy of Darlene M. and Edmond H. Guerin, Jr.

The Liberty Jencks Watering Trough stood on the farm, known also as the Garrison House, located in Abbott Run. Simon Wilkinson, another son of Jeremiah Wilkinson, the famed inventor of Ashton, lived in the house as well. Postcard circa 1908, courtesy of Elizabeth Allen.

87

The Diamond Hill Ski Run in 1957, at the height of its popularity as a ski resort. It has been closed for years but the town has plans to reopen the area as a park. Photo courtesy of Dea MacKinnon.

The first youth hostel in Rhode Island was at Diamond Hill. The building still stands as an outbuilding behind a private residence on Diamond Hill Road. The tavern was located in the front of what is now St. John Vianney Roman Catholic Church and was demolished in 1967. A training center for professional boxers was also in this area during the 1920s.

Among the noteworthy fighters that trained in this camp was Bill Brennan for his bout against world heavyweight champion Jack Dempsey.

The schoolhouse had been located on Diamond Hill Road near Metcalf Drive and is no longer standing.

The Mount St. Rita Convent and Health Center had its beginnings in 1913 when the Sisters of Mercy bought the former Fiske Farm overlooking Lake Miscoe north of Diamond Hill. Outdoor stations of the Cross were constructed in 1946. Mercymount Country Day School was constructed on the five-

The gatehouse of the Diamond Hill Reservoir was raised ten feet in the 1960s and another ten feet in 1971. The gatehouse was rebuilt each time. 1910 postcard courtesy of James Booth.

hundred-plus-acre property during the 1960s.

Tower Hill Road is named for the Tower family who lived in the area off Diamond Hill Road. It is the site of Beacon Pole Hill (circa 1775) where an elevation of 556 feet gave an excellent site for the placement of a beacon pole during the American Revolution. An eighty-foot pole with an iron kettle in which tar could be burned was part of a colonywide system to warn the residents of a British invasion. It was one of four such beacons in the state. The Tower Hill Road area has some of the finest eighteenth-century houses in the town.

The Pavilion at the Diamond Hill Reservoir was still intact in 1908 when this postcard was created. Courtesy of Darlene M. and Edmond H. Guerin, Jr.

The Provincial House at Mt. St. Rita's Convent was built by the Sisters of Mercy on land that was formerly the Fiske Farm. Postcard circa 1915, courtesy of Darlene M. and Edmond H. Guerin, Jr.

The Holy Name Society, the Arnold Mills Parade Association, the Knights of Columbus, and the Club Juventude Lusitana are among some of the organizations which have sponsored parades in town since the turn of the century. This float is believed to have been in a Holy Name Society parade through the villages of Berkeley and Ashton, photographed about 1915. Courtesy of Robert Rowbottom.

A PICTORIAL ESSAY

Life in Cumberland Throughout the Years

The following pages are a photographic essay of people and places in the community that is Cumberland, Rhode Island. Many of these places no longer exist. So many people shared their wonderful memories with us that we felt it was important to preserve them for future generations. We hope that this serves to remind the people of Cumberland of the importance of remembering and preserving our history and our heritage.

The Blackstone River at the villages of Manville and Cumberland Hill is an excellent portrait of the dams built to harness its energy. Postcard circa 1907, courtesy of Eleanor Johnson.

This photo taken by Robert Rowbottom shows two turn-of-the-century ladies walking down Scott Road in front of the Scott homestead. The house was built in 1787 by Nathaniel Scott and the road was named for him.

A group of Cumberland people gather at Happy Hollow, so named for the rather boisterous parties held in the area after the millworkers quit for the week.

The Happy Hollow Pond as seen in a
postcard from 1900. Courtesy of Darlene M.
and Edmond H. Guerin, Jr.

A view of Arnold Mills from a photo taken
on April 5, 1900. Courtesy of James Booth.

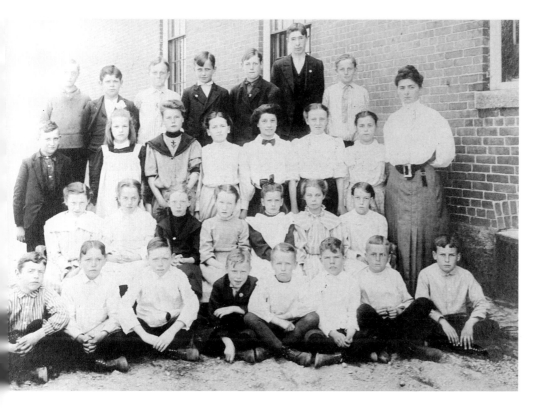

The children of Ashton School about 1925. Courtesy of the Angell family.

Ashton School children around the turn of the century. Courtesy of the Angell family.

Ashton School was constructed in 1850 with four classrooms, later serving as the school administration offices. It was turned back to the town in 1983. This photo probably dates from the turn of the century. Courtesy of Darlene M. and Edmond H. Guerin, Jr.

St. Patrick's Church was the second Roman Catholic church in the Blackstone Valley. It was built in 1860 in the village of Valley Falls. 1907 postcard courtesy of Darlene M. and Edmond H. Guerin, Jr.

ST. PATRICK'S CHURCH, VALLEY FALLS, R. I.

The parish church of St. Joseph's Roman Catholic Church was built in the village of Ashton in 1872. Postcard circa 1908, courtesy of Joseph E. Coduri.

The Berkeley Railroad Station in a postcard around 1910. Courtesy of the Angell family.

The Ashton Bridge was built in 1893 as a railroad bridge. Postcard courtesy of Darlene M. and Edmond H. Guerin, Jr.

The Valley Falls Railroad Station was constructed in 1877 as part of the Providence-Worcester Railroad. Cumberland had a flourishing freight and passenger service until the 1940s. Limited freight service still exists in some part of the town. Photo circa 1910 from the collection of the Cumberland Town Hall.

Opposite: The Valley Falls Fire Station was built in 1887 on Broad Street. It served the community until a new station was constructed on High Street. Postcard circa 1910 courtesy of Darlene M. and Edmond H. Guerin, Jr.

The parochial school of St. Patrick's Church in Valley Falls was built when the original church was constructed in 1861. The church was totally rebuilt in 1936 and the school was rebuilt in 1961 into the brick edifice that now stands on Broad Street. Post-card circa 1900, courtesy of Darlene M. and Edmond H. Guerin, Jr.

The Arnold Mills School, in the Cargill school district, operated until the construction of Community School in 1924. Photo circa 1900, courtesy of Elizabeth Allen.

The C. F. Perkins Store located in Arnold Mills was also known as the Walcott General Store and Dr. Halsey Walcott's Office. Built around 1819, it was operated as a general store well into the twentieth century. Postcard circa 1910, courtesy of Darlene M. and Edmond H. Guerin, Jr.

Presidents Day in what is believed to be the interior of the Club Juventude Lusitana in Valley Falls. Photo circa 1920, courtesy of Robert Rowbottom.

Armistice Day in 1922 at the Club Juventude Lusitana, a Portuguese Club located in Valley Falls. Courtesy of Martino Baptista.

The Cumberland Town Poorhouse was located on the grounds of what is now Cumberland High School on Mendon Road. The poorhouse cemetery was relocated for the construction of the school. 1960 photo courtesy of Martino Baptista.

The Arnold Mills Methodist Church and its two historic cemeteries (numbers 22 and 23) are located on Nate Whipple Highway. The cemeteries are still operated by a Cemetery Association which oversees all burials and upkeep. Photo courtesy of Jean Schofield Madden.

The Peck Cemetery located on Abbott Run Valley Road dates back to at least 1754 and is considered the earliest local graveyard. It contains the graves of many early families including the Ballous, Pecks, and Whipples. Postcard circa 1908, courtesy of Elizabeth Allen.

Mary and Annie Atkinson pose at the Tennison House. Photo circa 1910, courtesy of Louise Potter.

The Follett Homestead, shown in 1896, is one of the oldest images in this book. Photo courtesy of Stuart Follett.

The Cormier Homestead dates from 1896. Courtesy of Roland Cormier.

The Whipple Jenks House dates from 1850. The house was owned by Liberty Whipple Jencks and Ann E. (Rawson) Jenks. Courtesy of Katie McKenzie.

The basement of the Whipple Homestead, in the village of Ashton, was used as the Ashton Post Office. Postmistress Abbie L. (Ballou) Whipple is shown here with her daughter Ellen M. (Whipple) Angell and her children Emily, Evelyn, Charles, and Frederick Angell. Courtesy of the Angell family.

The Franklin House in 1907. Postcard courtesy of William Rhodes (Rhody) Franklin.

This house is located in Arnold Mills. Courtesy of Jean Schofield Madden.

Opposite page top: The N. W. Lee Homestead on New York Avenue near Bear Hill Road is seen here in 1898. The Lees ran a vegetable stand near the Chapel Four Corners area. Courtesy of Carolyn Kelly.

Opposite page bottom: The N. H. Lee Vegetable Stand stood in the area of the Chapel Four Corners as seen in this photo from October of 1939. Photo from Carolyn Kelly.

*The Stearns House on the
falls at Arnold Mills.
Margaret Stearns was a
benefactress of the entire
community. 1945 photo
courtesy of Scott Welton.*

*The Littlefield House in
Diamond Hill typifies the
architecture of that village.
Mr. Littlefield is believed
to have been a superintendent of a local cotton
textile mill. Postcard
courtesy of Jean Schofield
Madden.*

A turn-of-the-century family believed to be the Howards. Courtesy of William Rhodes (Rhody) Franklin.

The village of Arnold Mills is seen in a photo shortly before the fire which destroyed the Metcalf Mill. Photo by Robert C. K. Snow, circa 1980.

This house at 3170 Diamond Hill Road was built in the 1700s. Photo courtesy of Susan Howard.

A cottage on Blackstone Street in the 1890s. Courtesy of Vicki Large.

The Brindle House at the corner of Old Angell Road and Mendon Road circa 1925. Courtesy of the Angell family.

The McKee homestead in the early 1900s was located on Dexter Street. Courtesy of Thomas Pryor.

Opposite page top: Walker's Hardware Store in 1947. Courtesy of Marilyn Holden.

Opposite page bottom: The soda fountain at Gaskin's Pharmacy, which was located on Broad Street, is shown here about 1898. Photo courtesy of Ezekiel Cardozo.

Opposite page top: The interior of Gaskins Pharmacy shows the display cases containing cigars and other sundries. Photo circa 1898, courtesy of Ezekiel Cardozo.

Opposite page bottom: The Loucas and Miranda Grocery Store was a thriving operation during the 1940s. Photo courtesy of Barbara Luiz Hampson and Helen Bailey.

Below: The Loucas and Miranda Grocery which was located in Valley Falls. Photo circa 1940, courtesy of Barbara Luiz Hampson and Helen Bailey.

HANLEY'S Ale

GRAND OPENING of NEW WAREHOUSE
McLAUGHLIN & MORAN INC JUNE 4-1937
CUMBERLAND HILL R.I.

The McLaughlin-Moran Banquet celebrated the opening of their new warehouse in Cumberland Hill in 1937. The warehouse sold Budweiser beer products in the area for the better part of the twentieth century. Photo courtesy of John J. McLaughlin.

The grocery store at 17 Rawson Road in Arnold Mills is the present home of Kay Langille Faria. 1900 photo courtesy of Herbert Preston.

GROCERIES

This photo of the Blackstone building in Valley Falls in the early 1900s includes the streetcar and wagon, the transportation of that era. From the collection of the Cumberland Town Hall.

The first Cumberland Rescue truck was presented to the town by the Cumberland Lions Club during the 1950s. Photo courtesy of Patrick Mandeville.

The fire warden and firefighters of Valley Falls pose during the 1950s. Photo courtesy of Samuel and Hugh Ward.

Opposite page: Note the spires of St. Joseph's Church in the background of this photo of a butcher wagon in the village of Ashton. Photo circa 1890, courtesy of Louise Potter and Mary Geddes.

A 1920 Waterman Ford with William and Gordon Loynds in 1920. Photo courtesy of Raymond Loynds.

McKee's Super Service Station in Valley Falls during gas rationing in 1942 was a prelude to similar lines in the 1970s. Photo courtesy of Thomas Pryor.

The Cook Hotel in Cumberland Hill was prominent until the early 1900s, but no longer exists in the village. Photo courtesy of Arthur Colwell.

A dairy farm was located on Sneech Pond Road in the village of Cumberland Hill. Leo Raymond, Sr., age seventeen, delivered the milk throughout the town in 1912. Photo courtesy of Eileen Raymond.

The Howard Grain Mill in Abbott Run was located in an ideal spot near the railroad. 1908 postcard courtesy of Elizabeth Allen.

A winter scene from 1944 was photographed near Smith's Esso Gas Station in Valley Falls. Photo courtesy of James Wright.

The McKee Gas Station was located at the corner of Dexter and High Street in 1942. Smith's Esso Station was on the competing corner. Photo courtesy of Thomas Pryor.

Another view of Smith's Esso Station in 1937 in Valley Falls shows the dirt roads and treelined streets of the area. Photo courtesy of Thomas Pryor.

*Fred Shea and James McKee wait beside the gas pumps of yesteryear at McKee's Gas Station
on Dexter Street. A 1925 Model T. Ford is on the right. Photo courtesy of Thomas Pryor.*

Top photo: The freight station at Abbott Run is shown around the 1890s. Photo courtesy of Herbert Preston.

Bottom photo: The passenger station at Ashton Village. Postcard circa 1907, courtesy of the Angell family.

The Arnold Mills Railroad Station. Photo circa 1910, courtesy of Jean Schofield Madden.

John Long and Fred Voelker around 1900 at the railroad crossing in Abbott Run. Courtesy of Eva Schofield.

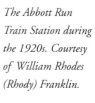

The railroad station at Grants Mill in 1912. Photo courtesy of Eleanor Johnson.

The Abbott Run Train Station during the 1920s. Courtesy of William Rhodes (Rhody) Franklin.

Ramp for the Ice House on Rawson Road in Abbott Run around 1910. Photo courtesy of Eleanor Preston.

The Conway Ice House in the 1920s on Sneech Pond. Courtesy of James Conway.

Ice Harvesting in 1916. Photo by Robert Rowbottom, courtesy of Kenneth Rowbottom.

Ice House on Rawson Road around 1910. Courtesy of Eleanor Preston.

This trolley took five hours to reach its destination in Providence during this snowstorm in the 1920s. Photo courtesy of Walter Gelinas.

The Pumping Station No. 2 on the Blackstone River at Valley Falls. Postcard courtesy of Darlene M. and Edmond H. Guerin, Jr.

The Keach and Brown Company and the Hesse Manufacturing Company were located in Valley Falls. Postcard courtesy of the Guerin family.

The Berkeley Mill Executives pose in 1939. Courtesy of Louise Potter.

Hilda Johnson Loynds works at her loom in the early 1900s. Courtesy of Virginia Loynds.

This farm wagon was photographed in 1915 off Scott Road by Robert Rowbottom.

The Johnson Farm in Abbott Run in 1962. Courtesy of Jean Johnson.

Howard Grainmill truck in the 1920s. Photo courtesy of Eva Schofield.

A farm in the Diamond Hill Reservoir area of Cumberland in 1970. Photo by Thomas Letourneau.

E. Whiting residence and barn in Grants Mill in 1896. Courtesy of Eleanor Johnson.

136

John S. Angell and his carriage in the 1900s. Courtesy of the Angell family and Allyn Jackson.

John McLaughlin, Sr., with his tenants, the Chicoine family, on a farm on Staples Road in 1915. Courtesy of John J. McLaughlin.

The James E. Angell Valley View Farm in the snow in 1944. Courtesy of the Angell family.

The Doire farm house was moved down Pound Road in the 1970s. The Doire farm was one of the last to utilize horses for plowing. Photo by Lisa Hindle Deppe, DVM, courtesy of Gerard Doire.

The James E. Angell Farm with cows on the unpaved Angell Road circa 1920. Photo courtesy of the Angell family.

The Lussier family of Cumberland Hill on the site of what became the barbershop in the area. Emma Lussier, Alexandrina (Mrs. Frank) Lussier, and Lena Lussier in front of the house on Vivian Avenue and Governor Street. Courtesy of Theresa Lussier.

James E. Angell (right), his son, Fred E. Angell (center), and his son-in-law, Fred L. Bascombe (left), process corn on the Valley View Farm in 1915. Courtesy of the Angell family.

A 1922 Pierce Arrow truck in front of the Howard Grain Mill in Abbott Run. Photo courtesy of William Rhodes (Rhody) Franklin.

Fred E. Angell and Charles E. Angell worked at Valley View Farm in Ashton. 1920 photo courtesy of the Angell family.

A hand manufactured tractor in use at the McKee Farm in Valley Falls in 1940. Courtesy of Thomas Pryor.

Egerton Farm on Scott Road was photographed in 1915 by Robert Rowbottom. Courtesy of Kenneth and Jack Rowbottom.

The Doire Family Farm in Cumberland Hill around 1940. Photo courtesy of Gerard Doire.

Top photo: An example of a delivery wagon from the Valley View
Farm. Note the name J. E. Angell, Ashton, on the side of the carriage.
Courtesy of the Angell family.

Bottom photo: The Charles E. Angell home was moved to make way
for the new Angell Road in 1930. Courtesy of the Angell family.

Right photo: The north side of the Angell Farm, shows the cherry trees
which gave the area its name, Cherry Hill. Courtesy of the Angell
family.

A Doire Family hay truck in 1940 on Pound Road, Cumberland Hill. Photo courtesy of the Doire family.

The Whipple Jenks House in 1850 located on Diamond Hill Road was reputed to have been a blockhouse during the King Philip's War (1675–1676). Courtesy of Kathleen Field.

Children helping with hay were captured in this photo by Robert Rowbottom about 1930. Courtesy of Kenneth Rowbottom.

The James E. Angell Farm was also called Valley View Farm, on Angell Road, Ashton. Note the crooked electrical pole along the unpaved road. Pre-1930, courtesy of the Angell family.

Ashton Village children play after the 1938 hurricane hit Rhode Island. Photo by Robert Rowbottom, courtesy of Kenneth Rowbottom.

A walking horrible strides through the Arnold Mills Fourth of July Parade in 1949. Photo by Ed Nelson.

Walking at the Arnold Mills Bridge in the early 1900s. Courtesy of Eva Schofield.

This float in a parade in Berkeley Village has the
Berkeley Methodist Church in the background.
Photo by Robert Rowbottom, circa 1915,
courtesy of Kenneth Rowbottom.

Robert McKee and a friend pose on the running
board of his car. Courtesy of Thomas Pryor.

People gathered in 1905. Courtesy of Mrs. John Sherlock.

The Willing Workers Society of the Lonsdale Primitive Methodist Church pose for this photo around 1915. From left to right are: E. Platt, A. Woods, E. Proctor, L. Platt, L. Carten, A. Harwood, J. Johnson, and L. Taylor. Courtesy of Ruth Bascombe.

Ladies pose about 1900 on the steps of the Cumberland Grange No. 2 in Arnold Mills. Courtesy of Eva Schofield.

The Ashton Cornet Band from Ashton Village, Cumberland, Rhode Island around 1913. Photo courtesy of the Angell family.

Young Master Gordon Loynds in 1920 with his pony. Photo courtesy of Raymond Loynds.

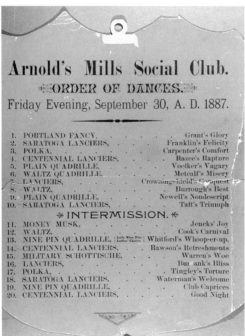

The Arnold Mills Social Club Order
of Dances, September 30, 1887.
Poster courtesy of Herbert Preston.

The Reverend Norman Vincent Peale (center in suit) visited a home in Berkeley in the later years of his ministry. The two residents have not been identified. Photo by Robert Rowbottom, courtesy of Kenneth Rowbottom.

The Arnold Mills Social Club Order of Dances, September 30, 1887. Poster courtesy of Herbert Preston.

Opposite page: Award winning photo shot by Albert Maurer about 1920. Courtesy of Louise Potter.

A canoe ride in 1920s Cumberland. Courtesy of Louise Potter.

Top photo: Fishing off the Abbott Run Bridge are, from left to right, Halsey Rawson, Edward Jencks, George Austin, and Henry Carpenter around 1890. Courtesy of Herbert Preston.

Bottom photo: The Manchester United Odd Fellows Hall, on John Street in the village of Valley Falls, is shown around 1908. Postcard courtesy of Joseph E. Coduri.

Miscoe Lake around 1910.
Courtesy of Eleanor Johnson.

Howard's Pond in Abbott
Run around 1910. Postcard
courtesy of Jane Wood.

A group play cards in Ashton in 1941. Photo by Robert Rowbottom, courtesy of Kenneth Rowbottom.

From left to right: Billy Wood, Walter Leslie Schofield, and David Long gather at Sadie Long's house located near the grange. Schofield later became the traveling freight agent for the New York/New Haven Railroad. Photo courtesy of William Rhodes (Rhody) Franklin.

Play ball! The Boston Nationals versus Berkeley at the Berkeley Oval in 1908. Postcard courtesy of Joseph E. Coduri.

In the grandstand of Berkeley Oval circa 1908. Postcard courtesy of Joseph E. Coduri.

The Ashton Football Club had a winning season around 1913. Courtesy of the Angell family.

The Lonsdale Primitive Methodist Church Championship Soccer League in 1917. Lonsdale Primitive Methodist Church collection, courtesy of Ruth Bascombe.

The old Colonial Bakery in the village of Lonsdale in Cumberland. 1938 drawing by Mildred Laxton-Kelly.

The Blackstone League Baseball all-stars about 1920. Courtesy of Louise Potter.

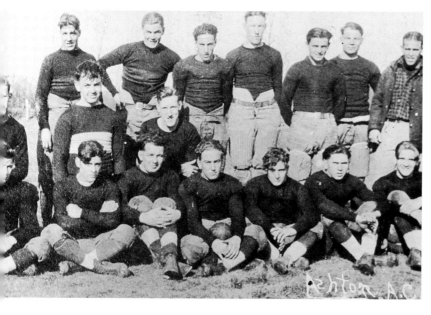

The Ashton Athletic Club football team around the 1940s. Courtesy of the Angell family.

Traveling in style in Ashton around 1910. Photo by Robert Rowbottom, courtesy of Kenneth Rowbottom.

Top photo: The T. J. Murphy Carriage around 1910 in the village of Ashton was probably decked out for the Fourth of July. Photo by Robert Rowbottom, courtesy of Kenneth Rowbottom.

Bottom photo: William Rawson of Abbott Run in his sulky in 1923. Photo courtesy Eleanor Preston.

Right photo: William Rawson and his friends about 1900. Courtesy of Eleanor Preston.

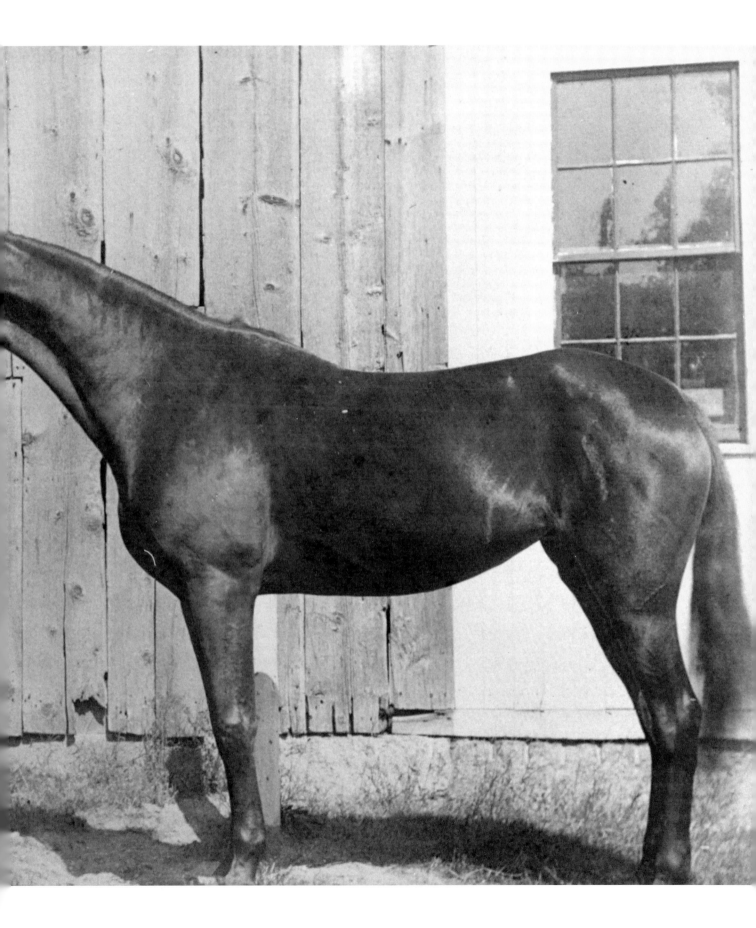

The Lonsdale Speedway in the southern part of Cumberland, shown here around 1954, provided years of fun to local residents. Courtesy of Stanley Stowik.

This aerial view of the Lonsdale Speedway shows the Ann and Hope Mill visible in the background. Circa 1954, courtesy of Stanley Stowik.

This car raced about 1954 in the Lonsdale Speedway owned by Bill's Auto Parts. Courtesy of Stanley Stowik.

The races at Lonsdale Speedway around the 1950s. Courtesy of Stanley Stowik.

Top photo: Sledding down Store Hill Road in Ashton Village in 1916.
Photo by Robert Rowbottom, courtesy of Kenneth Rowbottom.

Bottom photo: Joseph and Ruth Billington on the grounds at the Governor
Henry Lippitt Mansion around 1925. Courtesy of Joseph Billington.

Opposite page: Robert Rowbottom photographed these children near Scott
Pond around 1920. Courtesy of Kenneth Rowbottom.

Opposite page: Saluting the flag, children in Ashton honor their country in 1916. Photo by Robert Rowbottom, courtesy of Kenneth Rowbottom.

Right photo: Joe Charland's Tap Cafe in Cumberland Hill around 1930. Photo courtesy of Paula Vadenais.

Bottom photo: Arthur E. Howard photographed the Howard family around 1897. From left to right are: George Washington Adams Howard, his wife, George Howard, his wife Sarah Cargill, Horace Howard, his wife Jenny, Myrtle Alden Howard, and her husband Arthur Elsworth Howard. Courtesy of Doris Palmer.

Paper boys and friends gather before hawking the news in Ashton Village. Probably The Evening Times, the paper's headlines relate war news from the front during World War I. Photo by Robert Rowbottom, courtesy of Kenneth Rowbottom.

The Sixth Anniversary of the Club Juventude Lusitana was celebrated in 1927. Photo courtesy of Barbara Luiz Hampson and Helen Bailey.

Opposite page: Cumberland "Plein Air" landscape painter Charles W. Hirst (1875–1942) was an important contributor to the chronicling of nine-teenth-century Cumberland. His pictures depict the farms and homes of his native village of Ashton as in this circa 1938 painting of Angell Road before it was paved. The front building no longer exists, however, many of the other homes and businesses still stand. Courtesy of George Deignan.

This Hirst painting shows the Ashton mill houses, the Ashton Mill, and the Ashton Train Station. Painting circa 1938; courtesy of Jack Rowbottom.

AFTERWORD

It is hoped that this book in some way contributes to and enriches the lives of the people of Cumberland. Many hours have been spent gathering the information and photos to bring this book together.

One important message which its authors wish to leave with the readers is the need to preserve what is left of the historic buildings and places in the town for generations to come. All too many of our unique buildings and open spaces have been lost to our children. To reclaim some of our abandoned sites and preserve them for future residents would seem a wise course of action. We wish those who endeavor to save these places the best of luck and give them our thanks.

TIMELINE

History of Cumberland Chronology

Before the English settlement, the first people to inhabit the land of Cumberland were the Native American tribes of the Narragansetts, Nipmucks, and Wampanoags. They found the land forested by white oak, red oak, red maple, gray birch, American chestnut, hickory, and white pine.

1600s

1634: William Blackstone settles in what is now known as the village of Lonsdale in Cumberland. He is the first non–Native American settler in the state of Rhode Island and Providence Plantations. (He precedes Roger Williams into the state by one year.) The Blackstone River was named in his honor and has had an important place in the history of Cumberland.

1661: Wamsutta, called Alexander, son of Massasoit, chief of the Wampanoags, sells to Capt. Thomas Willett a deed to Rehoboth North Purchase, which includes the present towns of Attleborough and Cumberland.

1666: Capt. Willett conveys to the town of Rehoboth the land that comprised the North Purchase.

1676: "Nine Men's Misery": remnants of Capt. Michael Pierce's company are killed by the Indians and buried in one grave on what later become the Cistercian Monastery grounds (now the Edward J. Hayden Library grounds).

1700s

1720: Benjamin Walcott builds "Colonial Cottage" on Sneech Pond Road, which is now Nate Whipple Highway. (Although the home may actually have been built in the late 1600s, Benjamin is credited with its construction.) His son, Benjamin S. Walcott, served in the American Revolution and subsequently (circa 1818) owns weaving mills at Abbott Run. Another son, John, serves as a private in the Smithfield and Cumberland Rangers under the command of Capt. George Peck in October of 1777. John then serves as captain of the First Company of Cumberland Militia in 1792 and 1793. He was a member of the Cumberland Town Council and the Rhode Island General Assembly, and ran a general store and mill at Arnold Mills. Since John lived in Colonial Cottage, the home is also known as the "Captain John Walcott House" in the Arnold Mills Historic District.

1734: A sawmill is built in an area of what is now known as Arnold Mills. Amos Arnold purchases the sawmill in 1745. It closes in 1862. No remains are currently visible.

1736: Taverns open in Cumberland Hill.

1747: Cumberland, formerly called "the Gore," is taken from Attleborough, Massachusetts, and ceded to Rhode Island. It is incorporated as a separate town and included as a part of Providence County, Rhode Island. It has been called the "mineral pocket of New England."

The Arnold Mills Gristmill is constructed. It stands until 1962; its stone foundation and millrace can be seen today.

The Follett house on Tower Hill Road is an excellent example of an eighteenth-century home. During the American Revolution, Tower Hill Road was the location of the town's beacon pole, one of only four in the state. See the section on the village of Diamond Hill for more information. 1968 photo courtesy of The Times.

1749: The Elder Ballou Meeting House is erected near Iron Mine Hill. This hill is the source of many boulders of the official state stone (Cumberlandite), which were carried south over a large portion of the state during the glacial period. Destroyed in 1966 by vandals, the Meeting House was a gathering place for members of the Six Principle Baptist Society, which was organized in 1732. The Elder Ballou Meeting House, the first congregation of its denomination in northern Cumberland, was named for its pastor, Elder Abner Ballou.

Circa 1775: Beacon Pole Hill is utilized for a warning system during the American Revolution. The highest point in town at 556 feet, the eighty-foot beacon pole has an iron kettle that would be set alight to warn colonists of the British. It is one of four such signals in Rhode Island.

1777: The first agricultural newspaper in America, entitled *American Farmer*, begins in Cumberland.

1795: Cumberland Catholic Baptist Society builds a church in Cumberland Hill.

1800s

1800: Elisha Waterman and Benjamin Walcott build a cotton mill—the second one in America—at Robin Hollow.

1809: The Friends Meeting House, now the Arnold Mills Community House, is built in the Arnold Mills area of Cumberland.

1812: The General Assembly grants a lottery of $12,000, the proceeds of which are to be used in searching for coal in Valley Falls, Cumberland.

1818: Joseph Grant erects Grant's Mill, a saw and grain mill, in the area of Lake Miscoe, Grant's Mill, Cumberland.

Built in 1760 as the Eben Ballou house, this home was moved in 1803 to its present location at 2745 Diamond Hill Road and is known as the "House by the Side of the Road." Marion, William, and Grace Schofield are standing with Jean Schofield Madden (sitting on the lawn) in 1925. Courtesy of Jean Schofield Madden.

Crawford Titus erects the Happy Hollow textile company.

1823: The Cumberland National Bank opens in Cumberland Hill. It is authorized to create its own scrip. It closes in 1885.

1824: The Daniel Wilkinson house is constructed in Ashton. John Angell, who married into the Wilkinson family, later owns the property.

1825: The Metcalf Machine Shop is erected above the falls of the Abbott Run. Originally, it makes machinery for cotton mills. It is owned by Joseph and Ebenezer Metcalf. More recently, the building is used to store grain, as a blacksmith shop, and as a wagon shop. It burns down in 1987.

1827: The Arnold Mills Methodist Church is dedicated "open and free to all denominations." Its Boy Scout cabin, called "Crawford Cabin" (for the Arnold Mills Parade founder, Rev. Horatio Crawford), is moved to the church site and dedicated in March of 1933. In 1993, the cabin is renamed the Crawford-Johnson Boy Scout Cabin to also honor Clint Johnson, an active Arnold Mills resident and Arnold Mills Parade Association founding member.

1849: The Blackstone Canal closes, and its charter is revoked.

1850: The Valley Falls School and the former Ashton School (on Mendon Road) are constructed. The Valley Falls School is turned over to the town in 1979. The former Ashton School, which had become the Cumberland School administration building, is given back to the town in 1983; it currently houses the Cumberland Crime Stoppers.

Circa 1852: Harvey Chace, Samuel B. Chace, and Oliver Chace incorporate the Valley Falls Company. The following year, they construct a large stone dam near the Blackstone River at Valley Falls.

1860: St. Patrick's Church is dedicated in Valley Falls. It is the second Catholic church in the Blackstone Valley. It is remodeled in 1936.

Construction begins on the Lonsdale Company's new mill in Lonsdale, Cumberland.

1861: The former Cumberland Hill School, located on the corner of Mendon Road and West Wrentham Road, is constructed. It remains open as a school until 1971, after which it becomes a storage facility. It is turned back to the town in 1981. It is later sold to a commercial developer; it has begun a new life as an office building.

1868: The Lonsdale Company builds St. John's Episcopal Church.

A milldam is constructed at Manville.

1869: A part of Cumberland is incorporated as the Town of Woonsocket.

The Rhode Island Horse Shoe Factory (Union Horseshoe Factory) relocates to Valley Falls, Cumberland. It operates until 1914. The building still stands.

The Lonsdale Company erects a mill in the village of Ashton. It produces cotton textiles until 1935. In 1941, the Owens-Corning Company purchases the mill to manufacture glass fibers. It has been converted to a commercial apartment complex with new and modern living facilities for several hundred people.

1872: Construction begins on St. Joseph's Church on Mendon Road in the village of Ashton. The church is one of the finest examples of late Victorian, wooden religious buildings in Rhode Island.

The Brown and Ives Company constructs the Berkeley Mill, becoming the second largest textile company in the state of Rhode Island.

The Berkeley and Blackstone schools are constructed. The Berkeley School is given back to the town in 1981; the Blackstone School is turned back to the town in 1982.

1874: The Abbott Run Valley Bridge is constructed over the Abbott Run on Spring Street.

1875: A milldam at Arnold Mills is built.

1877: The Providence-Franklin Railroad, with a stop at Reservoir Road in Diamond Hill, is completed.

1882: The John F. Clark house, a unique Queen Anne–style house owned by the longtime Cumberland town clerk, is erected on Broad Street. The same company that designed this house designs the Cumberland Town Hall several years later.

The Boston Bridge Company builds the Church Street Bridge over the Providence and Worcester Railroad in Valley Falls.

1885: The Friendly Sons of St. Patrick Clubhouse is built on Broad Street in Valley Falls.

1886: The Boston Bridge Works constructs the Arnold Mills Bridge.

At approximately the same time, the Boston Bridge Works also constructs the Howard Road and Rawson Road bridges. These are among six extant truss bridges

The Berkeley Mill has undergone many transformations since this postcard was made in the 1920s. Courtesy of the Angell family.

built by this firm in Cumberland and among a small number of such surviving bridges in the state.

Engineer Frank P. Sheldon builds the Ann and Hope Mill for the Lonsdale Company.

1887: Cumberland Grange No. 2, the first grange in northern Rhode Island, is organized with a building constructed in 1895 at the corner of Abbott Run Valley Road and what is now called Arnold Mills Road. The building is now a private residence.

The Diamond Hill Reservoir is completed, and a new dam at Happy Hollow is also finished. In 1927, a new reservoir at Arnold Mills is completed. From these two reservoirs, by way of the Abbott's Run Stream, the water runs down into the Robin Hollow Pond, then into the Happy Hollow pond at Valley Falls, where a Pawtucket Water Works pumping station is located. These supply the water for Pawtucket and the lower Blackstone Valley.

The Valley Falls Fire Station and the United States Post Office are opened in Valley Falls. The post office later becomes the Valley Falls Library. The fire station is now a private business.

Lonsdale Primitive Methodist Church is organized under the leadership of Rev. John Proude.

1889: The first Cumberland High School is built on Broad Street, on what is now the site of the B. F. Norton School. The original building houses high school students until 1961 and closes to all students in 1985. It is rebuilt as the B. F. Norton Elementary School (named for former superintendent of schools Bernard F. Norton) in 1994.

The Berkeley Methodist Church is organized in the village of Berkeley. It should be noted that it is the first pastorate for Rev. Norman Vincent Peale.

Cumberland town clerk John Francis Clark (1854–1939). The town clerk was the most respected person in the government as he/she was responsible for all of the town's legal records. Mr. Clark served as clerk from 1888–1889 and again from 1893–1909. Photo courtesy of Irving Knight.

The Razee School House stood at the corner of Scott Road and Little Pond County Road (as it appeared in the 1890s). Photo courtesy of Gerald Razee.

1891: A strike in the Berkeley Mill occurs.

1894: The Cumberland Town Hall is erected on Broad Street. This is the first Cumberland building constructed specifically as a town house, and it is built on land previously owned by the Valley Falls Company. (The name "Town Hall" refers to a meeting room inside the Town House, but it has since come to refer to the entire structure.)

1895: The Providence and Worcester Railroad Station is constructed by the railroad to serve Valley Falls.

1899: The Cumberland Grange publishes the *Gleaner*, a monthly agricultural newspaper, until 1907.

1900s

1900: Nine members of the Trappist Order start the Cistercian Monastery, located on Diamond Hill Road. The town acquires the building and lands following a fire in 1950. The town library is established there in 1975.

1902: Clark Street School is constructed. The wooden building is turned back to the town in 1981. It no longer stands.

1903–1905: Dr. Lucius F. C. Garvin of Lonsdale Village, Cumberland, is elected governor of the state of Rhode Island. The Garvin house still stands on Broad Street.

1904: Berkeley Fire District is incorporated.

1908: St. Mary's Russian Orthodox Church is constructed in Cumberland Hill. It is the first Eastern Orthodox church in Rhode Island. Its name is later changed to Dormition of the Virgin Mary Orthodox Church.

Circa 1910: A one-story, wood-frame grain storage shed is built on Sneech Pond Road in Arnold Mills. The building has been rehabilitated and, since 1989, has housed a restaurant and small store.

1912: Nathan W. Whipple, Jr., purchases Metcalf Mill at Arnold Mills from Neil MacKenzie.

1915: The Broad Street Bridge is built; it connects Cumberland to its neighbor, the city of Central Falls.

1920: "Grayrock," a huge stone mansion that is now a private residence, is constructed off Angell Road by Squire Senior Nicholson, the president of a large supermarket chain.

Circa 1922: Electricity comes to Arnold Mills.

1924: Community School is built in Arnold Mills. Its classes replace those held in a one-room schoolhouse that still stands near the North Cumberland Fire Station.

A Cistercian monk at the Abbey of Our Lady of the Valley. Postcard circa 1940 from the collection of Gloria Carr.

The Naushon Company Mill was located in Valley Falls and featured in this postcard circa 1908 from the collection of Joseph E. Coduri.

Highland View Farm, in the area near Diamond Hill known as Grant's Mill. 1908 postcard from the collection of Joseph E. Coduri.

1925: Central Grammar School, located in Valley Falls, is built. It closes as a town school in 1994.

The one-room Arnold Mills Schoolhouse is given to the North Cumberland Fire Department for use as a firehouse. Community School, located on Arnold Mills Road (formerly Whipple Road), officially opens.

1926: The nation celebrates its 150th birthday (the Sesquicentennial) with parades in Providence, Bristol, and (in all probability) Chepachet (Glocester) and Cumberland. Providence's parades include a "Parade of the Ancients and Horribles," giving inspiration to Chepachet's and Arnold Mills' subsequent versions.

1927: Rev. Horatio Crawford of the Arnold Mills Methodist Church organizes the first recorded Arnold Mills Fourth of July

View of Valley Falls Pumping Station. Postcard circa 1910 from the collection of Darlene M. and Edmond H. Guerin, Jr.

Parade. It is preceded by a bonfire, which precipitates the flooding of the new Arnold Mills Reservoir.

1928: The Masonic Temple building is erected on Broad Street. It currently has a new life as Blackstone River Theatre, a center for the performing arts.

Circa 1930: Diamond Hill State Park is established as a recreational site. The town acquires the site from the state in 1992.

Garvin Memorial School is constructed on Diamond Hill Road.

1931: The North Cumberland Fire Department takes over the Arnold Mills Parade as a means to celebrate the holiday and collect funds to help support the department's service to the community.

Cumberland Hill Fire District is incorporated.

1932: The George Washington Park is created in front of Chapel Four Corners. It is designed to commemorate the bicentennial of the birth of the first U.S. president.

1934: Construction begins on the Ashton Viaduct (George Washington Highway). It concludes in 1945.

1946: The North Cumberland Fire Department erects a new fire station.

1950: A devastating fire destroys the church and some of the buildings at the Cistercian Monastery.

1954: Cumberland Hill Elementary School opens on Manville Hill Road.

Top: The George Howard home on Abbott Run Valley Road. Postcard circa 1910 from the collection of Darlene M. and Edmond H. Guerin, Jr.

Bottom: The old stone house, owned by the Heaton family, that was torn down to make room for the Grand Trunk Railroad. Photo circa 1913, courtesy of the Angell family.

Top: Scouts off camping in 1916 in the Ashton area, from the lens of renowned photographer Robert Rowbottom. Courtesy of Kenneth Rowbottom and the Rowbottom family.

Bottom: A working farm at Arnold Mills in the 1950s. The village was known to support boat builders, carriage repair shops, farms, and milliners, as well as a variety of other businesses. Photo courtesy of Dea MacKinnon.

1959: A new Ashton Elementary School is constructed on Scott Road.

1961: A new Cumberland High School is erected on the site of the former Cumberland Town Poorhouse. The poorhouse cemeteries are relocated to make way for the school.

1962: Construction begins on Sneech Pond Road, site of the Arnold Mills Parade. The new road is eventually named in honor of Nathan W. Whipple, Jr., who had been chief of the North Cumberland Fire Department since 1925. To make way for the new road, the Carriage Repository located across the street from Walcott's Store (which still exists) in Arnold Mills had to be destroyed.

1963: Our Lady of Fatima Parish is organized in Valley Falls. The first pastor is Rev. Albino Martins.

1966: Edward J. Hayden, former town engineer, is made the first town administrator of Cumberland in June of 1966. He serves in this capacity until March 24, 1978. He dies on July 19, 1978. Francis Stetkiewicz replaces Mr. Hayden as town administrator, and then becomes the first mayor of Cumberland when the town passes its new town charter.

1969: Cumberland Middle School is built on Highland Avenue.

1971: North Cumberland Middle School is constructed on Nate Whipple Highway.

1975: The Edward J. Hayden Library is dedicated at the site of the old monastery property.

Circa 1980: Construction of the Providence Zen Center at the former summer residence of Thomas P. McCoy, mayor of Pawtucket, on Pound Road, Cumberland Hill, begins.

Views of the John Street Bridge demolition from the north and south. The Lonsdale Drive-In Theatre was a popular spot in the 1950s for residents from both Cumberland and neighboring Lincoln. Photos courtesy of Everett Simpson and M. Wood.

1987: A fire destroys the Metcalf Mill in Arnold Mills, Cumberland. It was the last remaining mill in the area.

1992: Cumberland acquires the site of Diamond Hill State Park.

1997: To celebrate its 250th year of incorporation as a town, this history is published.

Top left: Buildings known as the "Widows Block" on the Blackstone River. 1920 photo by Robert Rowbottom, courtesy of Kenneth and Jack Rowbottom.

Top right: The Jason Cargill house on Abbott Run Valley Road in the 1950s. At one time, the Howard family owned the home. Photo courtesy of Doris Palmer.

Bottom: Lonsdale Sports Arena after Hurricane Edna (September 12, 1954). The arena was located in the area where a shopping plaza exists today, across from One Mendon Road, Cumberland's senior housing. Photo courtesy of Bernard Wallace and Leon Duquette.

Top left: Blackstone Valley Explorer plies the Blackstone River along Cumberland's riverfront.

Top right: Present Cumberland mayor David Iwuc in his alter ego, Captain Crime Stopper, on the Crime Stoppers Float in the 2002 Arnold Mills Fourth of July Parade. Photo courtesy of Beverly Perry.

Bottom: Militia groups in front of the Colonial Cottage during the Arnold Mills Fourth of July Parade. 2002 photo courtesy of Beverly Perry.

TOWN CLERKS OF CUMBERLAND

Job Bartlett	1746–1748
Daniel Peck	1748–1750
Uriah Jillson	1750–1751
John Dexter	1751–1786
Jotham Carpenter	1786–1799
John Rogers	1799–1804
Stephen Joslin	1804–1830
Pardon Sayles	1830–1842
Lewis B. Arnold	1842–1854
Pardon Sayles	1854–1855
William B. Arnold	1855–1865
Francello G. Jillson	1865–1867
Samuel Fessenden	1867–March 1870
John L. Clark, pro tem	March 1870–June 1870
Horace A. Follett	1870–1887
Patrick F. Kinion	1887–1888
John F. Clark	1888–1889
Patrick F. Kinion	1889–1893
John F. Clark	1893–1909
Joseph V. Broderick	1909–1934
Stephen A. Fanning	1934–1951
John J. Conway	1951–1970
Agnes T. Teal	1970–1982
Frances M. Audette	1982–1987
Ronald G. Graveline	1987–1989
Roberta A. Hitchen	1989–1990
Marianne B. Mulholland	1990–2000
L. Jean Simoneau	2000–2004
Patricia Skurka	2005–

HISTORIC CEMETERIES IN CUMBERLAND

The following is a list of historic cemeteries in the town of Cumberland. Adapted from
The Valley Breeze, June 15, 1996

Number One: St. Patrick's Cemetery, located on High Street, 1,000 burials, 100 veterans, mid-nineteenth century

Number Two: St. John's Ukrainian Cemetery, located on Hewes Street, 80 burials, 4 veterans

Number Three: Cumberland Cemetery, located on Dexter Street, 500 burials, 38 veterans

Number Four: Old Cemetery, located on Dexter Street, at the corner of Curran Road, 2 burials

Number Five: St. Basil's Cemetery, located on Curran Road, 300 burials, 42 veterans

Number Six: Mt. Calvary Cemetery, located at Curran Road, 1,000 burials, 70 veterans

Number Seven: St. Joseph's Cemetery, located at Mendon Road, undetermined number of burials, 134 veterans, late nineteenth century

Number Eight: Ballou Cemetery, located on Old Mendon Road and Scott Road, unknown number of burials, 42 veterans, early nineteenth century

Number Nine: St. John's Episcopal Cemetery, located at Old Mendon Road (rear of St. John's Parish House), 150 burials, 59 veterans

Numbers Ten and Eleven: Former Brown-Bartlett and Bartlett (Former Poor House Cemetery) Cemeteries moved when the current high school was located on Mendon Road

Number Twelve: Carpenter Lot Cemetery, located on Mendon Road in front of Cumberland High School, undetermined number of burials, late eighteenth century

Number Thirteen: Weeden Cemetery, located on Nate Whipple Highway, 8 burials in a crypt, no veterans

Number Fourteen: Staples Family Lot, located on Nate Whipple Highway, 18 burials, no veterans

Number Fifteen: Pickering and Staples Lot, located at the corner of Staples Road and Nate Whipple Highway, 25 burials, no veterans

Number Sixteen: Peck Cemetery, located at Abbott Run Valley Road, 300 burials, 49 veterans, mid-eighteenth century

Number Seventeen: Metcalf Cemetery, located at Abbott Run Valley Road, 50 burials, no veterans, mid-eighteenth century

Number Eighteen: Quaker Cemetery, located at Abbott Run Valley Road, 75 burials, no veterans

Number Nineteen: Evergreen Cemetery, located at Nate Whipple Highway near Arnold Mills Methodist Church, 250 burials, 6 veterans

Number Twenty: Arnold Mills Cemetery, located on Nate Whipple Highway, near Arnold Mills Methodist Church, 400 burials, 11 veterans, mid-nineteenth century

Number Twenty-one: Old Diamond Hill Cemetery, located on Reservoir Road, 500 burials, 18 veterans, mid-nineteenth century

Number Twenty-two: New Diamond Hill Cemetery, located on Reservoir Road, 200 burials, 17 veterans, mid-nineteenth century

Number Twenty-three: Weatherhead Family Lot, located on Mayflower Drive off Womantan Lane, 12 burials, no veterans

Number Twenty-four: Elder Ballou Meeting House Cemetery, located on Elder Ballou Meeting House Road, 500 burials, 11 veterans, eighteenth century

Number Twenty-five: Whipple Cemetery, located on Elder Ballou Meeting House Road, 25 burials, 1 veteran

Number Twenty-six: Wilcox Family Lot, located on Old Manville Road, 13 burials, no veterans

Number Twenty-seven: Scott Lot, located off West Wrentham Road in the woods, 12 burials, 2 veterans

Number Twenty-eight: Wilkinson Cemetery and Tomb, located on Angell Road behind the Calvin Presbyterian Church, 35 graves, no veterans, early nineteenth century

Number Twenty-nine: Kimball Lot, located between Willis Avenue and Kimball Street in Colwell Acres, 65 graves, no veterans

Number Thirty: Cook-Carpenter Lot, located on Plantation Street near Apache, 16 graves, no veterans

Number Thirty-one: Resurrection Cemetery, on West Wrentham Road, undetermined number of burials

BIBLIOGRAPHY

SECONDARY SOURCES:

Boucher, Susan M. *The History of Pawtucket: 1635-1976.* Pawtucket, R.I.: Connecticut Printers, 1976. Available through the Pawtucket Public Library.

Conley, Patrick T. *An Album of Rhode Island History, 1636–1986.* Virginia Beach, Va.: The Donning Company, 1986.

Cumberland, Rhode Island: Progress 1950. Democratic Town Committee, 1950.

Rhode Island Historical Preservation Commission in cooperation with Cumberland Historic District Commission. *Historic and Architectural Resources of Cumberland, Rhode Island.* 1990.

Glocester, The Way Up Country. Town of Glocester, R.I.: The Heritage Division Glocester Bicentennial Commission, 1976.

Haley, John W. *The Lower Blackstone River Valley: An Historical Narrative.* Pawtucket, R.I.: E. L. Freeman Co. Lower Blackstone River Valley District Committee of The Rhode Island and Providence Plantations Tercentenary Committee, Inc., 1937.

Hayden, Edward, ed. *Cumberland, Rhode Island: Historical Story.* Town of Cumberland: n.p. Third Edition, January 1976.

Jencks Ray, Judith. *Founders and Patriots of the Town of Cumberland, Rhode Island.* Baltimore, Md.: Gateway Press, Inc., 1990.

McLoughlin, William G. *Rhode Island: A History.* New York: W. W. Norton and Co., 1986.

Palin, Raymond. "Revolutionary Cumberland: A Note on a Historical Controversy." Rhode Island Historical Society Publication, Nov. 1993, pp. 129-134.

Simpson, Robert V. *North Cumberland: A History.* Randolph Center, Vt.: self published, 1975.

Woonsocket: A Centennial History—1888–1980. Woonsocket, R.I.: Woonsocket Centenial Committee, 1988.

PRIMARY SOURCES:

Conway, Eugene R. "As It Looked to Grandfather." 1994, 2 pp.

Cormier, Roland. "The Cumberland Bank 1823–1865; The Cumberland National Bank 1865–1885." 12 pp.

Crawford, Rev. Horatio H. Diary. Arnold Mills Methodist Church, 1922–1931.

Furnace Carolina Site (Arnold Mills Furnace). National Register of Historic Places, April 1993.

"History of Town of Cumberland." Cumberland High School, 1947, 44 pp.

Howard, Arthur Ellsworth. "My Father: George Washington Adams Howard—A True Story of Rugged Individualism." Privately published, 1953, 49 pp. Now in the collection of Doris Howard Palmer, Cumberland, R.I.

Jackson, Allyn. "Recollections of Ashton and Berkeley." Cumberland, R.I., 1996, 86 pp.

Knight, Irving W. "Information on John Francis Clark and the Currier Mansion." 1996, 3 pp.

Laxton-Kelley, Mildred. "The House That Hezekiah Built." Unpublished, in the collection of the author, 1992, 13 pp.

Woika, Michael. "History of Dexter Clark and the Dexter Clark House." 1995, 14 pp. Available through the Cumberland Public Library.

PERIODICALS:

The Providence Journal Bulletin, published in Providence, R.I.

The Times, published in Pawtucket, R.I.

The Call, published in Woonsocket, R.I.

The Valley Breeze, published in Cumberland, R.I.

Many thanks to the following contributors of photos and postcards for this book:

James Acciolli
Elizabeth Allen
Lee Allison
Dorothy Angell
James Angell
Susan Angell
Helen Bailey Dubois
David Balfour
Martino Baptista
Ruth Bascombe
Joseph Beck
John Bessette
Joseph Billington
James Booth
Luann Bower
Patricia Bradley
Ezekiel Cardozo
Gloria Carr
Gordon Carr
Fay Catterall
Joseph E. Coduri
Arthur Colwell
James Conway
Roland Cormier

Patricia Costa
Lou DeFusco
George Deignan
Gerard Doire
Leon Duquette
Marie Fleurant
Stuart Follett
William Franklin
Norman Galipeau
Mary Geddes
Walter Gelinas
Mary Grigas
Darlene M. Guerin
Edmond H. Guerin, Jr.
Barbara Luiz Hampson
Samuel Hindle
Lisa Hindle Deppe
Marilyn Holden
Susan Howard
Allyn Jackson
Eleanor Johnson
Jean Johnson
Carolyn Kelly
Mildred Laxton Kelly

Henry Klos
Irving Knight
Vicki Large
Thomas Letourneau
Janet Levesque
Raymond Loynds
Virginia Loynds
Theresa Lussier
Dea MacKinnon
Jean Madden
Patrick Mandeville
Lucille Martin
Katie McKenzie
John McLaughlin
Edward Nelson
Doris Palmer
Beverly Perry
Louise Potter
Eleanor Preston
Herbert Preston
Thomas Pryor
Eileen Raymond
Gerald Razee
George Rose

Jack Rowbottom
Kenneth Rowbottom
Robert Rowbottom
Eva Schofield
Dot Scott
Mrs. John Sherlock
Everett Simpson
Claire Smith
John Smith
Robert C. K. Snow
Stanley Stowik
Thomas Turner
Gertrude Tuscher
Paula Vadenais
Bernard Wallace
Hugh Ward
Samuel Ward
Scott Welton
Jane Wood
Mary Wood
James Wright

And also:
Cumberland Public Library
The Times

The following contributors have submitted invaluable information in the form of unpublished memoirs/articles for this book:

Ruth Bascombe: "Lonsdale Primitive Methodist Church: 1887–1995"
Ezekiel Cardozo: "The Catholic Institute"
Eugene R. Conway and James E. Conway: "As It Looked to Grandfather"
Roland Cormier: "The Cumberland Bank 1823–1865, The Cumberland National Bank 1865–1885"
Allyn Jackson: "Recollections of Ashton and Berkeley"
Mildred Laxton Kelly: "The House That Hezekiah Built"
Irving W. Knight: "John Francis Clark"
Raymond Palin: "Revolutionary Cumberland: A Note on a Historical Controversy"
Doris Palmer: unpublished book by Arthur Ellsworth Howard "My Father—George Washington Adams Howard: A True Story of Rugged Individualism"
Michael Woika: "History of Dexter Clark and the Dexter Clark House"

INDEX

ABOUT THE AUTHORS

Joyce A. Hindle Koutsogiane, Ed.D. earned her doctorate in Educational Leadership from Boston University in 1992. She is a school administrator in the Town of Cumberland, and is a former English and theatre teacher. She is a longtime Cumberland resident and serves as chairperson of the Cumberland 250th Anniversary Commission. Since 1988 she has been parade chairperson of the Arnold Mills Fourth of July Parade.

David W. Balfour is president of D. W. Balfour Associates, a firm which specializes in the advertising and publishing fields. He is chairperson of the Cumberland Historic District Commission and serves on the Rhode Island Historical Preservation and Heritage Commission. He serves as chairperson of the Board of Directors of the Blackstone Valley Tourism Council and is a member of the Cumberland 250th Anniversary Commission.